novum pro

James **Kubik**

THE AWAKENING OF I

novum pro

www.novumpublishing.com

All rights of distribution, including via film, radio, and television, photomechanical reproduction, audio storage media, electronic data storage media, and the reprinting of portions of text, are reserved.

© 2021 novum publishing

ISBN 978-1-64268-202-1
Editing: Karen Simmering
Cover photos: Michael Ludwig, Oleg Doroshin | Dreamstime.com
Cover design, layout & typesetting: novum publishing

www.novumpublishing.com

ACKNOWLEDGEMENT

Many years ago a friend of mine, Ivette Reyes Campbell, had a dream of writing a book named "The awakening of I." Recently Ivette asked me if I would like to use the name for my book. I felt that was the most perfect name for this book because it relates my awakening and hopefully yours.

I would like to thank my brother, Tony Kubik, and my sister, Susie Kubik, who pushed past the doubt and believed in me. I am sure it was a difficult task, but it goes on to show that all things are possible. Good luck on your journey through this life.

Most importantly, I would like to thank Sherry Keefe. I never met anyone who could say all that needed to be said by saying nothing at all. I still don't know how you do it, but your support of my writing this book is astounding, and I appreciate you more than my words can say.

Chapter One

THE AWAKENING OF I

I went to a Catholic grade school, and I was pretty sheltered from the outside world. My entire world consisted of about eight blocks and back home. When I graduated grade school, my parents asked me if I wanted to go to a Catholic high school or a public high school. I wanted to go to a public high school; after all, that was where all my friends were going. At the very least I would know someone at this new school. Little did I know that I would consider this new school a new universe. I was definitely out of my element. I didn't fit in anywhere, and my old friends moved on to new friends. I definitely had low self-esteem, and finding new friends did not come easy. It was so easy to smoke pot or drink to be accepted in this new world. I did make one new friend, but looking back now, my new friend had no idea what friendship was. I'm sure he was happy to have a tag-along buddy. This guy was so much more worldly intelligent than I was, and I was so naïve about the world, I would follow him anywhere. My parents tried to warn me about my new friend, but come on, what did my parents know? Not much that I could see at sixteen.

I remember when I was sixteen years old my mother wanted me to watch this show that came out called "Scared Straight." It was about these young teenagers like myself who happened to be on the road to destruction; my friends were questionable too. It was obvious that my parents could sense that I was one of those who needed to see the show. On the show, these young teenagers were brought to prison and the inmates did their absolute best to scare these teenagers so they would re-evaluate their lives and friends and straighten out. I watched that show, but it was too late; the show didn't affect me at all. I was above all that, and I certainly wouldn't get caught doing anything wrong.

At fifteen I was introduced to drugs. At sixteen I figured out that my parents didn't know anything and my friends knew a whole lot more. It was just so much easier to smoke pot and drink or do harder drugs then to do the things my parents wanted me to do. Like working and going to church and helping out around the house. What teenager wants to do that when we can go out and have fun, meet girls, hang out with friends and get high? After all, we only have one life, so why waste it doing boring things? I often wonder if teenagers or young people in general are like me and have this mental block that disables them from listening to anybody except their friends. At the age I am now, I'm all for listening to people and the advice they have for me. I can accept or reject what they are saying; at least I realize I am not the all-knowing young man I once was and what they have to say could be important to me. I have become smart enough to know that I don't have to live through every situation to learn from it. I can learn from others and what they have gone through. This has saved me a lot of heartache.

The road that everybody travels down is different than the one that I've traveled down then and now. What is important to know is that ONE MISTAKE IN YOUR LIFE CAN AFFECT YOU FOR THE REST OF YOUR LIFE, AND IT USUALLY DOES. I can easily say the life that teenagers and people in general live now is drastically different than the life that I lived as a teenager in the 1970s.

It just seems to me that the life we now live is spinning out of control. What we thought was important then has been replaced with what is important now. Rightfully so; each generation changes, and what worked then may not work now, but *one thing that has never changed is the way that God loves me and the way that God loves you*. I know what you're thinking: *Here's another God saved me story*. Sure enough, but give me a chance – better yet, give God the chance to open your eyes because I know a secret.

It's not time for the secret now because you have to know a few things about me. Once all the drugs and alcohol left my system, my conscience was bothering me, and I was angry. I knew better; at least I was supposed to know better. It seemed to me that when I didn't do drugs, I could easily say no to anything that was wrong and I had a higher resistance to people who wanted me to do anything wrong. When I was high I couldn't say no. I needed the approval of my peers or my so-called friends. I was miserable because I thought I was supposed to be miserable and I was going to stay that way forever. I hated myself. I tried to kill myself numerous times because that was the only way to make up for my past.

I have since figured out that THERE IS NO WAY POSSIBLE TO MAKE UP FOR YOUR PAST. If there was, I would have found it by now. If you do something wrong to someone, no matter how sorry you are, it doesn't take away the wrong that you did. The wrong does not go away. Even if you are forgiven for the wrong that you did, it still doesn't go away. Since there is no way to make up for your past, you have to find a way to let it go or believe that there is a higher _power_ or the universe itself that can help you live peacefully with this baggage that we all insist on carrying around with us.

For twenty-five years, I was miserable. I would not allow myself to feel happiness, I would not even watch a comedy show on television. I wanted to be miserable. I made my own conscious choice to be miserable, and no one was going to change my mind. Fast forward: After twenty-five years of misery, I called my parents and said *I can't do this anymore. I can't be miserable any longer. Twenty-five years is enough! There has got to be some reason to be happy, to find a way to live with this past of mine.* Hence the first step on my road to recovery. My misery was not over yet; it was true that I had trained my sub-conscious brain to always see the negative. I convinced myself that in every situation I had to figure out all the bad things that could happen, and then what did happen was usually not as bad as what I was thinking. I felt like I was living multiple lives; first with all the bad things that *could* happen, and secondly what really did happen. This was truly miserable, but it was the process that I lived by. It was the only thing that would work so life would not be so bad. In all actuality, it was worse. I was living a hundred different negative lives to my one real life. I had just moments of happiness here and there. For example, there might be something funny on television, or you might lift more weights at one time than you ever have before, and you feel a level of accomplishment.

    I was so miserable that I truly believed that there was a battle going on in the world between good and evil and for sure evil had won. I was in the deepest hole of despair, and I couldn't dig my way out. I couldn't believe why, if there was a God, why was I still alive? It would have been more merciful for me to die. I had no will to live, so I definitely was the perfect candidate for the graveyard. I refused to have hope. Hope was just another way to hurt yourself. Who made hope anyway? Why is it there? I cannot tell you the amount of times that I gave hope a chance and ended up regretting that decision. I can easily give you a hundred reasons why not to hope, and I can give you only one reason to hope: because God loves you. As negative as hope can be, on the other end of the spectrum, hope can be equally positive. Where there is hope, there is a chance for a positive life. There is power in hope, and hope leads to belief.

    Still, there was no end in sight for my misery, and what made matters worse was I kept seeing on the television all these ministers who were happy. It was a slap in the face to me. I'd prayed my brains out, and I was still miserable. What did they have and what was I lacking?

    I decided right there that I was going to give God one hundred percent; then when I was still miserable *I knew it wasn't my fault*. It was God's fault, and he was just a mean old God who didn't care or didn't exist. I dove right into reading and studying the Bible. None of it made sense, but still I read it. Then sure enough, I got knocked down. *I knew I was right*. I'd given God one hundred percent and still I was down here in the hole of despair… I started thinking that maybe it wasn't exactly one hundred percent. I had to admit that maybe it was eighty percent. So I would give God another chance to get right with me. *Hey, I'm doing the best I can, so now I can show God how to be merciful.*

What was happening was that God was rescuing me from being in this unhealthy situation. I was going to church, reading my Bible, and doing whatever I could to give God my one hundred percent. I even started a Bible course in the mail. *Now I know I'm on the right track – what more can I do?* I went to college, and I got a degree and diplomas in horticulture and custodial maintenance. Then whack, I got knocked down again. *What the heck? I'm in trouble again.* Now I knew I'd given God one hundred percent. *I don't understand, I'm getting in trouble and it's not even my fault…* Well, was I really giving God a hundred percent? Maybe it was ninety percent? Not only that; I had the opinion that if I gave God one hundred percent, then nothing bad would happen to me, and I could breeze through life with no problems. Now I know that bad things in life happen to everybody, regardless of your beliefs.

I decided right then that the hair-like thread that was connecting me to God would not be broken. I knew inside that if I believed my life would work out, then I could be happy. Then all of a sudden, because of the Bible course, I started to understand what I was reading. I ran across a verse in the Bible that states, "My brethren, *count it all a joy* when you fall into various trials." (James 1:2) Well, that's just crazy. *Count it all a joy?* Who does that? Maybe I didn't understand anything. Someone who has had nothing but trials their whole life is not going to count any trial a joy! *Okay, I'll give it a shot.* When I fell into any trial, I started saying *Thank you, God, for taking me though this hardship. I don't want to go through this hardship, but I know something good will come out of this.* Funny thing is the trials started not to last as long, and I felt a peace while going through them. When I didn't thank God, the hardship lasted forever, or until I finally remembered to thank God for it. This concept of thanking God for the trials I was going through is definitely beyond my comprehension, yet it worked.

Romans 8:28 states that "And we know that all things work together for good to those who love God and are called according to *His* purpose." Was I called according to *God's* purpose?

Search me, but I felt comfort believing that someone like me can be called according to *His* purpose. How could anybody like me be called according to *His* purpose? Like magic, God started revealing things to me. One of the heroes of the Bible is a man called Moses.

We all know the story: Moses started off his life pretty roughly. He was born into a death sentence just for being born a boy (Exodus 1:16). His mother had to give him up to save his life by floating him down a river in the hopes that the pharaoh's daughter would have mercy and save him. Thankfully, their plan worked, and Moses was saved. When Moses was grown, he came across an Egyptian beating one of his fellow Hebrews. "So he looked this way and when he saw no one was looking, he killed the Egyptian and hid him in the sand." (Exodus 2:12) Moses committed a murder and buried the body.

It is hard for me to imagine that this man was chosen to lead the Hebrews out of Egypt and slavery, yet Moses became a fugitive instead. The king was out to kill him now, and Moses had to run, so he ran for forty years. Here we have a murderer who is a fugitive who is called one of the heroes of the Bible. *Well, there might be hope for me after all.* Moses went on to lead the Hebrew slaves out of Egypt. My point is that if God can use Moses to fulfill His purpose to lead the Hebrews out of Egypt regardless of the mistakes that he made, then I am sure God can use me with all the mistakes that I made. I needed to figure this out. I was a follower, and now no one was going to lead me where I didn't want to go. How could I let God lead me? Could I put so much trust into anybody or anything that my whole life would depend on it?

When God wants a hundred percent, He is not joking, but there are promises that go along with giving Jesus one hundred percent. Hebrews 13:5 states "Let your conduct be without covetousness; be content with such things as you have. For He Himself has said, *'I will never leave you or forsake you.'*" Hey, that sounds like a promise to me.

What about those times when I feel like God has forsaken me after all I've been through? There have been an awful lot of times where I felt like God had forsaken me. I suppose I can think of those times as a reminder of how good it is when I'm doing what it takes to keep myself humbly grounded in God's love and how bad it feels like when I am out of God's good graces. By the way, did I thank God for taking me through this hardship?

I received a lot of flak for trying to turn my life around. People don't want you to better yourself. Some people assume that you think you are better than them just because you are trying to better yourself. I understand now that the way people respond to your success will tell you how they are dealing with their own life. I refuse to let that affect me. I now understand that it is the same all over the world: People don't want you to better yourself. The truth is that you haven't changed; you are still you, and it is their jealousy or their lack of courage to become a better person that has changed their point of view of you. Besides that, *everyone has a right to have an opinion, just like you have the right to accept or reject that opinion. You have to be true to who you really are and stop trying to be who your friends want you to be. If you are worried about what your friends think of you, then you are in a prison of your own making.* I am not saying to be a selfish, conceited *It's all about me* kind of person. Friend or not, all people need to be treated with dignity, honor, and respect. I am saying that I have come to learn that *when someone in our lives wants us to go in a certain direction, and we know deep down inside that we shouldn't, this is a test and you have to want God's approval more than that person's.* I realized that if I have to change who I really was to be accepted by the people around me, then I wasn't being true to myself. At this point I was just starting to feel good about myself, although I knew I still had a long way to go.

Another thing that really stood out to me is that *what God wants for my life is a whole lot better than what I want for my life.* At this point I just wanted to get by without being in a physical or mental anguish prison, but my friends just wanted me to stay in the same rut that they were in. It's a no-brainer: I'll go with God's plan for my life. After all, being in the same rut as my friends is not going anywhere and hasn't worked out for me so well. Plus, I am not responsible for making my friends happy, and my friends are not responsible for making me happy. If it works out that way, then great. God gave all people a free will. Just as I made a conscious choice to be miserable, I can make a conscious choice to be happy. Everybody knows the saying *You can't please everybody.* The reason this is so true is because it's not your responsibility to make everybody happy. *It is your responsibility to treat all people with dignity, honor and respect.* You don't have to agree with their lifestyle or the color of their hair or how they choose to live their life. It is not our place to judge; it's our place to love all people. I am not saying to trust everyone you meet, because you will get hurt. People are human. It is easier to do the wrong thing, but it takes guts to do the right thing, and that is why more wrong things are being done.

To the people who rejected my going in a forward progressive motion, I can only hope that one day you figure out the secret. Oh yeah, the secret; I forgot about that. Well, we are well on our way to the secret. What the secret *isn't* is that if you have to see it to believe it, you're missing the point. There are going to be times in your life when you will have to believe it without seeing it. *You can visualize it in your mind and believe it.* The person who has cancer doesn't see the medication or the chemotherapy working; they just have to believe that it is working. They can visualize the medication working, which is better than believing it is not working. The Bible says that "Now faith is the substance of things hoped for, the evidence of things not seen." (Hebrews 11:1) When you have faith in God, that does not mean you get everything you want in life. If we got everything we wanted immediately, we would probably be in big trouble, because most of the time we don't know what is good for us and what isn't. There are just too many things going on at every second of the day. There is never nothing going on. Thankfully, there is always a delay in answered prayers. That way we can re-evaluate what is best for us or rely on the fact that God knows what is good for us and what isn't.

Even now, things don't always go right for me – go figure – but I did read where it says, "That you may be sons of your father in heaven; for He (God) makes the sun rise on the evil and on the good, and sends rain on the just and the unjust."(Matthew 5:45) Clearly, God plays no favoritism, and not many people go through life without anything bad happening to them, although some people get more bad than good. I wonder if it is because they are focusing on all the bad and forgetting all the good. If I had a choice, I would rather tap into this unlimited *power* source, this positive energy that teaches me that to be positive and hopeful is better than being miserable. Later on we are told, "But without faith it is impossible to please Him (God), for he who comes to God must believe that He is and that He is a rewarder of those who diligently seek Him." (Hebrews 11:6) Hey, that sounds like another promise.

I'll take that promise. I like being rewarded, and one thing that I can humbly say is that my life sure is going a lot better now that I am giving God that one hundred percent because of my belief. Am I giving God one hundred percent now? On most days, I would have to say no; there are far too many problems that affect me and I haven't been able to get ahold of yet. One thing is for sure: I cannot rid myself of this feeling that some of my problems are too big for me, and I have to rely on my higher power to solve them.

I think it is pretty fair to say that the hardest thing in life we will ever have to do is believe that all things are possible when there are nothing but negative things around you. It is hard to be thankful for the good and positive when we can't even remember what the good and positive is. It is almost as if we need to train ourselves to remember there are still good and positive things in our lives no matter what is going on. I'm pretty human, and I'm prone to make mistakes, so I'll have to keep on guard to keep giving God the Glory He deserves. Thankfully God knows I'm not perfect, and sure enough, I'll slip up somewhere along the line. Luckily for me, God is all merciful, so all I have to do is recognize where I slip up, make amends, and thank God for His forgiveness.

Used to be I would slip up and go through weeks of guilt asking God to forgive me multiple times, which was a waste of time! I learned the hard way that if I am sincere, God will forgive me the first time, so why trouble God with the guilt I am feeling for weeks after? That also means that I am denying myself the positive energy that God has for me. Essentially, I am punishing myself. If I do wrong and I am forgiven, why am I punishing myself? Wouldn't it be better to move forward and let my actions show that I regret my actions and I am not going to make that mistake again? I have come to realize that carrying around a mountain of guilt for something you have been forgiven for stops you from going forward, and the best way to show how sorry you are is to live your life in a positive way.

I was told that I need to live a good life. Well, a lot of good that does to the people in my life that were hurt by my actions. It doesn't seem fair. I get to live this good life while everybody else is miserable because of my actions. I humbly say that I am sorry I couldn't find a way to make up for my past. Please put your faith in the _power_ of God and know that it is time for you to be released from your misery prison. All things work for good to those who love God and are called according to His purpose.

Chapter Two
WHAT'S THE DEAL WITH FEELINGS?

I never thought that I would say this because I always believed that feelings don't control us. Now I believe that feelings are a God-given set of tools for us to use. Think of it as if we are born with a set of tools to be used at our disposal. Babies who are hungry or need their diaper changed use their emotions to tell us something is wrong. They do not know they are using their emotions; they just are. There is no law that says we have to stay in a certain mood. The good thing is since feelings are tools, then we can always put down the tool we are using and pick up the tool that would be better for us to use. For example, if you wake up in the morning on the wrong side of the bed and you are dreading the day, nothing seems to be going right. And you just woke up.

Right then, play your favorite song – music is very positive – remember the good things in your life, listen to an uplifting message, or write a song of thanksgiving. Say a prayer, give someone a hug, or read a Scripture from the Bible. Just do whatever it takes to get that right tool in your possession. Say to yourself *I don't need this negative tool right now, and I am going to use my good feeling tool to make my day go the way that I want it to go.* This puts you in control of your feelings, which in turn controls how your life goes. It is never all bad. Regardless of how you are thinking and feeling, there is still some good somewhere in your life. There has got to be in your life a system that keeps you tapped into the _power_ and energy of God and feeling positive. What is it? Only you can answer that.

Life is meant to be lived in an abundant manner. Abundance comes from living in the positive. There is a story in the Bible about two blind men who kept following Jesus, crying out and saying, "Son of David, have mercy on us." (Matthew 9:27) Jesus asked them if they believed that he was able to return their sight to them, and they responded, "Yes, Lord." Matthew 9:29 states, "Then he touched their eyes, saying <u>*according to your faith let it be to you*</u>." This verse is so important for us to understand. Jesus is essentially saying that we all can tie into the God-given <u>*power*</u> that exists in the world. Whether we love life, hate life, whether we are positive or negative, whether life is good or bad is totally up to us. Jesus has given us the <u>*power,*</u> and we can attract good or bad through the good and bad <u>*power*</u> that exists in the world.

Do you treat yourself the way that you want others to treat you? If you expect good things in your life, you will receive good things in your life. I know what you're thinking: *I have all kinds of negative things that happen to me.* Well, if you think that you are going to go through life with no bad things happening, you are kidding yourself. Bad things happen to everyone. The positive people who believe do not allow these bad things to push them over the edge of the negativity mountain. They understand that things happen, and it is a challenge to get around these things in a positive way. They are getting experience that will help them with the next problem, and it is all good. Positive people don't allow this thing that happened in their life to submerge them in the sea of negativity.

I noticed that in life we have a huge amount of people who like to judge. They do not like us because of the way we look, act, the music we like, who we know, what we eat, our sexual preference, the way we talk, and every other thing that you can think of. I personally have had people dislike me because I am a happy person. Little do they know that I was not always a happy person. I've had a difficult life. It is only because I choose to be happy that I am happy now. I believe that I deserve to be happy, and so I will continue to be happy. The successful, happy people don't allow the judgment of others to germinate and destroy them in their thinking. Most successful people do not allow negative judgments against them in. They don't need it; they are on a mission. Successful people pick up their joyful expectation feeling tool knowing that the bad things in life will pass, and they will move on to a sunnier day.

Take an inventory of your feelings toolbox. You have good and bad feeling tools:

- If you feel good, that means you're on the right track. Keep going; good things will come your way. Also remember this verse: "These things I have spoken to you, that in Me you may have peace. *In the world you will have tribulation,* but be of good cheer, I have overcome the world." (John 16:33) I would not go so far as to expect tribulations, but my free will allows me to choose to be of good cheer and gratefully expect that problems will not last forever.
- If you feel love, then keep that tool going. Let us say that you get into an argument with someone that you love. Are you going to stop loving them just because you do not agree on something? (No) Or are you going to continue to love that person despite your disagreement? Do not put down your love tool. There is a solution to the problem. Maybe the best thing is to step back and *don't think* about the problem and give your subconscious a chance to figure out the solution. I have notice that when I get around certain people I feel like my heart starts to beat again. I just feel good being around those people. They don't do anything special; they are just being themselves. That is what I call love, and that is a blessing.
- If you feel joy, then take a moment and get used to that feeling. Remember what it feels like. Expect it to come again. Feeling peace and joy is so much better than feeling any negative emotion, we should choose and strive for peace and joy.
- If you feel hope, then believe what you are hoping for you can achieve, that you deserve what you are hoping for. Hope is from heaven. Don't allow the negative feeling tools to sneak their way in and steal your hope.
- When you feel a passion for something, don't allow that passion to go by the wayside just because life is too busy. Find time to act on that passion.
- If you feel gratitude, then understand that you have tapped into the *power* of the universe. Nothing can bring you more

goodness than gratitude. I wonder what would happen if everybody kept a book that listed all the things that they were grateful for? If they went back and read all that gratitude list every day or every week. I bet they would realize that good things happen more often than they realized. For some reason it is not easy to remember the good things. We are always looking for what is next, and we do not fully take in the good that is happening right now. Right now, right here next to me I have a list of my top blessings. I see it every day, and I do not take my blessings for granted.

- If you feel positive and that brings on hope. For example if you are saying to yourself "I am very positive this is right for me," that brings on hope that you are on the right track and that you can accomplish anything. At that point it doesn't matter what your friends think. It is your duty to do what is right for you.

Feelings that you need to pay attention to but not allow you to control you are:

- If you feel worried, that is a warning about something… For example, if your friend wants to do something, but you don't feel good about it… take heed. It's a warning, and the consequences are what you are calling for. For every action there is a reaction; that is the law of the universe. But let's face it; some days we just wake up depressed. Some people can be depressed just because it's Monday. Put that tool down and pick up the tool that lets you feel good and positive. Monday is a glorious day. It is the new beginning of a promising week with plenty of blessings, and who would want to miss out on that? I know what you are thinking: *Well my life does not go that way; it does not happen for me. What can go wrong will go wrong.* Yes, you are right, think about it. The positive power of God, the positive power of the universe is only for those who believe and expect good things to happen. If you expect bad things, then don't be surprised when bad things happen. It is what you want and are calling for; otherwise, you would choose to change your outlook on life and let in the good things that are all around us. Furthermore if you are expecting bad things to happen, why can't you expect good things to happen?

- If you feel scared, it could mean danger. There is a lot to this fight or flight emotion, and every situation is different, so you will react different in every situation. I always try to trust my instinct on what the appropriate action should be. Usually I trust God to bring me through what I am afraid of. I would rather be tied into the power of the almighty than go through scary situations by myself.
- If you feel anxious, "Be anxious for nothing, but in everything by prayer and supplication, with thanksgiving, let your requests be made known to God." (Philippians 4:6) I have noticed that when everything is going good and I am flying high with the eagles, something will happen. I will sense that my flying high days are over because I just know that since things are going too good, it will just have to end. Hey, all good things come to an end, right? Wrong! My mother and father were married for sixty years, and they were true to each other all the way until they passed on. I come from a long line of extended marriages. Businesses have lasted for generations, and the freedom that you are experiencing right now in the United States has lasted since the year 1776. Good things don't have to end, but that does not mean that you will never experience some bad things along the way. We are not promised, nor are we entitled to a life of easy living, but we can choose to be happy along this journey called life regardless of the problems that will arise. We have had plenty of problems in this country along the way; it is the same with every business and even my mother and father's marriage. It is not easy to rid ourselves of this emotion called anxiety. Anxiety brings on depression and feelings of hopelessness. *Oh, Lord another mountain.* Thankfully, we are given a clue as to how we can rid ourselves of anxiety. Scripture says that we are to be anxious for nothing, but in everything by prayer and supplication,

with thanksgiving let our request be made known to God. By doing what this verse says we are in fact re-focusing from the anxiety to the solution to the anxiety. The answer is to refocus. Believe me, I know it is not an *I will snap my finger and I will be refocused* kind of deal. Yet it is possible, because when you refocus from the problem to the solution, you are in essence letting God know that you believe in His power and that you expect God to help you get past the problem and you are grateful that the problem will be solved. You also have no problem doing your part to get to that solution. Regardless of whether or not you want to admit it, God works behind the scenes in all of our life, which is why all things happen for good to those who love God and are called according to His purpose. The hard times anxiety are all just stepping stones to another level of awareness to beat the odds of being stuck in this negative pattern of life.

- If you feel lonely, then get around people who care for you. There is someone who has that unconditional love for you, and they want you to feel good about you. You owe them nothing in return, and they will not accept anything. Their payment is seeing your joy. People in general are a social bunch. We crave that human interaction, and a hug can go a long way. Thankfully there are social activities that we can attend. Church, parties, and get-togethers – society is full of activities, sports venues, and restaurants even have televisions so you can enjoy the company of people while watching your favorite team. One thing I know from personal experience is that no one wants to go home to an empty house or apartment. For me, that is the worst. I can get pretty stressed and my thought process brings on more negative thoughts. It is dreadful. I learned that there is no way to make friends in an empty residence. People may argue that point with the invention of the internet, but you don't get any human contact on a computer. It is a temporary fix.
- If you feel guilt, then figure out why, make amends to the best of your ability, and move on. I have had people tell me that

they feel guilty, and they did not even do anything wrong. You know what I say? Put down that tool you don't need right now and pick up your *I'm going to be happy* tool. Thank God I grew up in the Catholic Church, but sometimes I wish churches would not so much concentrate on guilt and fear – although this is important – but more on how good and powerful is this wonderful being who created this amazing world. That would be more advantageous. Let's face it; someone like me is never going to live up to the perfect being that I am supposed to be. I have too much negativity going on in my past, and from the looks of it tomorrow I will still fall short in my thoughts and in my words, what I have done and what I have failed to do. Being perfect is a mighty big order to live up to, and maybe I should be the best that I can. After all, if I don't live up to being the best that I can be, then I am only cheating myself of the life that God wants me to have.

- Resentment to me is a two-edged sword. When I feel resentment toward another person it robs me of my ability to see all the good qualities I appreciate about that person. My resentment will grow, and one resentment will lead to another resentment until I have a mountain of it. I realized that resentment was a useless emotion that can bury me under a negative cloud, and I couldn't see passed this negative cloud, to the clear blue sky that brought me happiness. So what was I to do with this resentment? Should I allow it to destroy my relationship? One thing that I learned is that I did not need to focus so much on this resentment, and if I was going to focus on anything I should focus on why I had this resentment. I mean, it wasn't there yesterday, so why is it there today? Here is where the second part of that two-edged sword comes in. I feel like my resentment was my way of pointing a finger at the person I was resentful toward because I didn't want to point my finger at myself and what was really wrong with me. In one particular incident I was mad at myself for not being farther along in my success as I felt I should have been, and I blamed this person because if they had done this, than I wouldn't have to deal with my shortcomings. My resentment was actually stopping me from the success that I feel like I ultimately deserve. I was stopping myself from getting what I want most of all, which is to tie into this free power that comes from Christ. The funny thing is that once I uncovered the real problem, I was not resentful any longer. The resentment went away, and I felt good about the person I'd had the resentment toward. There are other kinds of resentment too. If you feel resentment or anger; for example, someone says something about you that you don't like, don't focus on what was said. Let it go and pick up the tool that will keep you going forward. Does it really matter what someone says about you? Are they right? Why would they think that about you? Are you giving them the impression that is who you are? The only one you need to please is God, the one who has the _power_ to make your life all that you want it to be. Some friend or stranger that says something about you doesn't add up to much, and why would you let them get inside your head? Like I said before, if someone says something bad about me to you, don't even tell me; keep it to yourself. I don't need the criticism on the road that I am traveling. If you have constructive criticism, then by all means tell me because I want to be all that I should be.

It is amazing how many tools that we are born with. I have not even listed them all. What is even more amazing is that feelings are personal. We all have the same emotions, but those emotions are personalized to be used as we deem necessary. Something bad can happen to two different people, yet each person has the ability to pick up whatever feelings tool that they want to use at that time. I love driving, but at this time in my life I always seem to be behind the little old lady or little old man or the person texting on their phone who needs to go ten miles under the speed limit. Oh my God. I find it hilarious. I always think of it as God's way of telling me to slow down. I could get road rage, but then I would be behind a slow-driving person and I would be aggravated. Seems to me that I am doing better having one problem than having two problems. I'll pass them when I can or wait expectantly for another opportunity to be on my way.

Not too long ago I went to Tennessee. If you go there you will notice a church every half mile or so. I believe they call this the Bible belt, because the average attendance of people who attend church there is greater there than anywhere else across the country. I do believe the people there are friendlier and happier. I have never been called sweetie or honey more times in one day in my life than when I was in Tennessee. I went to a store there, and the girl behind the counter did not know that I was in a hurry. I was picking up some ceiling paint that was needed for a job I was doing. She just started asking me all kinds of questions about how to paint. Inside I was thinking, *Here we go… I don't know if I will ever get out of this store,* but I politely answered all her questions, listened to her story, and was out of there in like ten minutes. I do declare that I felt amazing inside. It was great. I was calm and relaxed. I was at peace. Later I realized that these people have the <u>power</u>. They understand that their faith in God is the tool that ties them in to the promises of God. They have every reason in the world to be happy, and they treat most every person that they run across like a friend. How cool is that?

Chapter Three
FRIENDSHIP

When you are in those teenage years, friendship is probably one of the most important things in your life. That and getting a car so you can drive to your friend's house. I have come to find out that most people don't really know what friendship is all about. This is sad because friendships are so important. I would be asked why I need to be so analytical about friendship, it's easy: People who get along are friends. I don't think anything in life is that easy. I have come to find out that friendships are few and far between. If you find a true friend then you are really a blessed person.

I would ask people what it means to be a friend. Many answers from many people would be that you would treat someone the way that you want to be treated. Sounds like a business deal to me. *Hey, I'll treat you well if you treat me well, let us shake on it.* Plus isn't that the golden rule? Treat people the way that you want to be treated. I do believe that you should treat people the way you want to be treated, but that is not friendship. It is part of your character; to have kindness and consideration for the next person should be a given.

Friendship is a one-way street. You can give someone your friendship, but there is no law that says they have to give their friendship back. There was this guy that I considered my friend. He would ask me for little stuff, a pencil, a cup of coffee, some ramen noodles? *Sure, here you go. I am glad I could help, that's what God would want me to do.* I never expected payback, and it's against my rules to owe anybody, so everything was good. Until the one time I didn't have what my friend was asking for. You would have thought that I'd done some major wrong to this guy. He verbally lit into me like there was no tomorrow. I was a lousy friend, I was greedy because I wouldn't share, and how dare I say no when he went through all the trouble of allowing me to be his friend.

Needless to say, our definition of friendship was on opposite sides of the spectrum. I had to find out what God's definition of a friendship was. From what I understand, God is a friend to all, and if anybody would know what a friend is, that would be God. So I started searching. I learned that King David wrote a psalm, and in it he wrote "The Lord is my Shepherd; I shall not want." Hmm. I never knew anybody that didn't want something before; is that even possible? Where is this going? 2 "He makes me lie down in green pastures; he leads me beside the still waters." Sounds like God is giving David peace. 3 "He restores my soul. He leads me down the path of righteousness for his name sake." Well, this could mean restoration for a weary soul from all the anxieties of the world. 4 "Yea, though I walk through the valley of the shadow of death, I will fear no evil: For you are with me; your rod and your staff, they comfort me." Now we are talking about protection. 5 "You prepare a table before me in the presence of my enemies; you anoint my head with oil; my cup runs over." Does this mean that God provides even during our darkest times? 6 "Surely goodness and mercy shall follow me all the days of my life; and I will dwell in the house of the Lord forever." David definitely humbly expects the _power_ of God's promises to provide all that he needs in this life forever and beyond.

Now I know why God is a friend to all. There was no agreement or written contract between God and David. *God in his friendship provided all that was in his _power_ to David.* This Psalm speaks of no particular thing that David did for Jesus; this friendship is a one-way unconditional love provision from Jesus to David. That is what friendship is: a one-way street. We can give our friendship to someone, but unconditional friendship says *you don't expect anything back*. True friendship is when you get that unconditional love in return. Unfortunately, that kind of friendship is rare, so when you run across it, hold on tight. David did write and acknowledge God's friendship to him. He was well aware that God was his friend, and David was God's friend; you can see it through his actions during David's whole life. David emulated God in his life, by showing mercy, compassion and love.

Plus he always acknowledged God whenever God worked in his life and gave God His glory.

When you read the other psalms that David wrote, you can see that he had a rough life too. David was either thanking God for his help, praising God for his glory, begging God for his protection from his enemies, or apologizing to God for the wrongs that he'd committed. David was definitely always trying to stay in God's good graces. David was a good rememberer of how many times God had saved him or blessed him or answered his prayer or forgave him for a wrong that David did (which were many). The point is that David knew that there was great _power_ in God, and that God loves to share His great _power_ to those who believe in Him.

The amazing thing is that whether we tie in to God's great _power_ is up to us. Just like David had the choice to have faith and believe in this unending _power_ source that we call God, we can make the right choice like David. We also have the choice to remember all the good things that God has done for us. With remembering comes a foundation on which to build. We start thinking, _Hey, God has helped us before; I'm sure God will help us again._ There is an expectation there for God's help. When you expect God to help you, that shows God that you have faith in Him. Faith is the tie that binds us to the _power_ of God. When you do not get what you want or God answers no to your prayer, what kind of friend will you be back to God? Will you get angry or be mad at God, or will you remember all the times God blessed you and say thank you anyway?

When you are dealing with friendship, it is wise to be more concerned with your own actions than that of the person you are friends with. I have a policy that I never forget what my friends do for me, and I never remember what I do for my friends. If I feel like I am being used instead of being in a friendship, I cautiously pull myself back, and I thank God that I had the power in me to be the type of friend that I learned about in the Bible. There are no regrets on my part.

You will know if you are being used by your friend. For example, if it feels like the person is sucking your life blood out of you every time they come around because they just want to complain and vent about everything and everybody, then this is a case that misery loves company. Time to back away. If the only time you hear from a friend is when they need something, it is time to back away. If you feel comfortable being around this person, and it is always positive and uplifting, you have a good friend. Friends build each other up, not tear them down. They listen, they care, and they are not afraid to tell you if you are wrong about something because they know the friendship is strong, and you would do the same for them.

Chapter Four

POWER

There is a Scripture in the Bible that says, "I can do all things through Christ who strengthens me." (Philippians 4:13) This Scripture is one hundred percent correct, but it is for those who already *believe*. When you believe you can do all things through Christ who strengthens you, you are saying that you are already tied into the <u>power</u> of God, and God will give you the <u>power</u> to sustain every difficulty and go through all of life's circumstances. When life is going good, this faith that you can, this belief that you are tied into this great <u>power</u> only makes life better, more abundant, and more prosperous. When I personally say this Scripture, I always say that I believe I can do all things through Christ who strengthens me. It is my reminder to stay tied into the <u>power</u> of God that God wants to share with me.

It may sound like I never go through any hardships. Believe me, I go through plenty of them When I am going through things that I don't understand, and I forget to pick up the right tool to help me get past the hardship, my negative attitude is full blown, and the <u>power</u> that exists in that negativity is beyond my control. It is like I can't stop thinking about it. I get angry at God because I believe God is supposed to help me – why isn't God helping? Just because God isn't helping me on my timetable doesn't mean that God isn't helping. So I pray and I thank God for this trial that I'm going through. I let God know that I don't want to go through this trial, but if I must then maybe there is a reason for it. I trust God for the reasons that are beyond my comprehension.

Years ago I stared my walk with Christ. I would have a lot of people vent to me. You know sometimes it's just nice to have someone to talk to especially in difficult situations. I would go out to talk and sometimes just walk or I would meet someone, and we would walk and talk. Once there was this one guy who was so mad at God that he would even go so far as to deny that God existed. His wife was leaving him, and his kids were acting up; there was just one problem after another. He was mad at God, yet he forgot that he'd made the decision to commit the wrong that lead to his problems. I would say, *Wow, this is so great.* He said, "Haven't you been listening to me? I'm dying here."

Yes, I was listening. *I can't fix the wife and kids part of your life, but I do wonder if God doesn't exist, why are you so mad at him?* You see, I understood the principle that in everyone God exists. I understand that we are made in God's image. Now I am not sure if God has two legs and two arms, a head and a torso. I believe the image we are made in is on a more molecular level with DNA and atoms and spirit. You may not want to consciously admit that God exists, but that feeling of anger toward God proves God exists, and He is going through the same pain that you are right now.

God doesn't want your wife and kids to leave you. Marriage vows are sacred. God doesn't want to see anybody going through pain and misery. God wants you to be happy and joyful and prosperous; that is why God made so many promises to us in his word. God gave us access to his *power* through Jesus to accomplish anything that we want. Sometimes we don't know what God's plan for our life is, but one thing is for sure: If you follow the teachings of Jesus, whatever you do you will succeed because God want us to be happy and successful just as we also want God to be happy and successful. Now you are tied into a true friendship with the One who matters. Besides that, what if God's purpose for your life is to be more like God? Maybe God wants you to use the *power* that He created the world with using only His words. What if you and I can create the life that we want by using the *power* of our words?

"God has spoken once, twice I have heard this: that *power* belongs to God." (Psalms 62:11)

"… The God of Israel is He who *gives* strength and *power* to His people." (Psalms 68:35)

"And do not lead us into temptation, but deliver us from the evil one. For Yours is the kingdom and the _power_ and the glory forever amen." (Matthew 6:13)

"You are mistaken, not knowing the Scriptures nor the _power_ of God." (Matthew 22:29)

"…And the _power_ of the Lord was present to heal them." (Luke 5:17)

"And the whole multitude sought to touch Him, for the _power_ went out from Him and healed them all." (Luke 6:19)

"Behold, I send the promise of my father upon you: but tarry in the city of Jerusalem until you are endued with the _power_ from on high." (Luke 24:29)

"But you shall receive _power_ when the Holy Spirit has come upon you…" (Acts 1:8)

"And what is the exceeding greatness of His _power_ toward us who believe, according to the workings of His mighty _power_." (Esp. 1:9)

"Finally, my brethren, be strong in Lord and in the _power_ of His might." (Esp.6:10)

"For God has not given us a spirit of fear, but of _power_ and of love and of sound mind." (2 Tim. 1:7)

"Behold, I give you the authority to trample on serpents and scorpions and over all the _power_ of the enemy and nothing shall by any means hurt you." (Luke 10:19) During this time, scorpions and serpents were symbols of spiritual enemies and demonic power.

"Then God said, "Let there be light," and there was light." (Gen. 1:3)

When you believe in this power, where this power comes from, (Matthew 19:26) and that this power is there for you to use, you tie yourself into a higher level of living. *I can* comes out of your mouth, and *I can't* does not belong to you any longer. The big question that we should be asking ourselves is why can't we? What is holding me back from success, from getting what I want in life? Do we not believe that we can? Do we not want to succeed because of the responsibility that comes with it? Are we just comfortable in our misery because we know it could be worse? My brothers, sisters, and I were brought up in such a way that the generation before us didn't want to rock the boat, and they handed down to us beliefs that are no longer relevant in the ever changing world.

I give myself permission to be happy right now. I will not be happy after I get everything I want, but I am happy on the journey to getting everything I want. If by chance I don't get everything I want, well, at least I was happy in my life, and happiness is very important. Most people say *I just want to be happy*. Okay, be happy then. What are you waiting for? Happiness is one of the feeling tools that we are born with. Pick up that tool and use it.

Well, if I had a better job or more money I'd be happier. Don't quit your job, but start dreaming of that job that will pay what you want. A better job and more money will come easier if you believe you deserve a better job, and more money will follow accordingly. Maybe you will get the promotion at the job that you work now.

There is a Scripture in the Bible that goes like this: "He gives *power* to the weak, and to those who have no might He increases strength." (Isaiah 40:29) Do you believe this is true? If you do not believe that this is true, then you are the cause for the limitation of God's *power* and the *power* that He wants to give to you, the *power* that exists inside of you. The *power* that exists in your words and the *power* that exists in your mind. If you do believe that this is true, then let me introduce you to a word in the Bible. The word is "Qavah" pronounced (Kah-vah) this word is used over fifty times in the Bible. It is a verb that means to wait for, look for, expect, and hope. Qavah expresses the idea of waiting hopefully[1]. I believe that if I wait hopefully and expect God's *power,* then when I need it in my life, that *power* will be there for me to use to get past anything life throws my way. Furthermore, I will continue to go in a forward progressive motion because of this *power* and continue to succeed.

---

1 New King James Bible Nelson 1252

Essentially, the Bible is telling us that God will provide the very best for us if we are willing to do our part by trusting and believing in Him. I have come to find out in my own life that there will be times that believing will not come as easily as others. It is at those times we must make up our minds to trust our higher power. What you believe has nothing to do with your feeling. Many times I have said to myself that I am just not feeling it, the doldrums have come upon me, yet I still made the conscious decision to go in that forward progressive motion and trust God. It appears to me that the closer we come to God and the belief that all things are possible, the more we are under attack from the negativities of life. We may be on the verge of a breakthough, and we do not want to suffer a setback just because our feelings have turned negative for no apparent reason or the things that we are expecting have not come yet or fast enough.

Thirty years ago, Lionel Ritchie and Michael Jackson wrote a song called "We are the World." The song was dedicated to help the people of Africa. In the song, there is a line that goes "There is a *choice* we are making, we are saving our own lives. It's true we make a better place just you and me." I can see that Lionel Ritchie, Michael Jackson and the others star singers who sang the song believed that they could make a difference – and a difference they did make.

The choices that we make in our everyday life can make a difference. Some days discouragement can set in. I mean discouragement that you cannot shake off of you; it just will not go away. You were expecting something, and it did not happen. Now you feel tired and let down; after all, you expended a lot of energy by hoping, praying, and believing. You just don't know how much longer you can take it. Maybe it's better to go back and not have high expectations; that way, you don't have to deal with being let down emotionally. On the other hand, it does feel kind of good to believe and hope in something and you did not really lose anything by doing it. The only thing is you are tired from expending that much energy. Now is the time to thank God for what you are feeling, put that trust and belief in the One who has the power to make everything better, and to pick up one of your feel good tools and have a great day.

You are still in control of how you feel, and there is no rule that says you have to feel bad. You did not do anything wrong, so there is no anxiety to deal with. Who says that just because you did not get what you were hoping for you have to have a bad day? Is what you were hoping for and wanting the best thing for you? Plus, isn't it true that you just did not get what you wanted and hoping for yet? Who are you to say that it is over, and you will not get it? Do you allow yourself to get frustrated because things are not working on your timetable? As a matter of fact, since you did not get what you were hoping for you should – with purpose – have a great day. People have to be as low as I was not to give hope a chance; otherwise you will one day hope and believe again. It is much better to hope and believe with a positive mindset than with a negative mindset.

If we understood that what we are feeling today is creating our future, we all would be on a mission to feel better. Every day I wake up and I am grateful. I literally say *Thank you, God, for this beautiful day and the blessing that you have in store for me. Today I know I am in for something good.* I feel good, I feel happy, and I usually don't have any problem until I run across someone who is angry because I am happy. Go figure, right? We appear to live in a world where it is okay to be mad at someone just because they are happy. When this happens, I can immediately see that this person is not happy with their own life, and they find it offensive that I am happy. So I tone down my happiness around them. I am very much happy inside, but I don't want to offend anybody. They are making a conscious choice to be unhappy. That is okay. I am not in charge of their happiness; I am in charge of my happiness. If being unhappy works for them, then more power to them. Being unhappy does not work for me. I find that I enjoy life much more being happy, positive, and grateful. How about you?

I believe I can see myself going places. Most of the time the road I am on is taking me up, yet if feels like I am going downhill.

I get to coast on my journey because I realize that if I focus on all the things that I do not want in life, I will sure enough get those things I don't want. So I choose to focus on the things that I do want. I am the creator of my own life, just like you are the creator of your life. I choose to believe in a loving God who wants me to be happy, prosperous, generous, and to live an abundant life. I know what you are thinking: *Yeah, but what if it does not work out for me that way?* The promises of God state that it will work that way. We all are going to experience ups and downs. Am I going to let the downs tailspin me to a mediocre life where I am just existing? Have I become comfortable in my misery because it is the only life I know? I am going to thank God for the downs; I believe that they are there for a reason. Then I am pressing forward to the life I love. What if it does work out for my advantage? Please, someone, explain to me the downfall of believing in an all-loving God?

For me to be successful, I do my best to never forget that God does turn negative situations around for our benefit. The power of God enables new doors to be open that would never open before. Regardless of life's ups and downs, I find it encouraging to believe everything will work out. I also realize that there will be times when I need to get mad dog mean in order to stop the negative obstacles that get in the way of my going in a forward progressive motion. These negative obstacles are usually in my mind, and they always start off with these two words: "What if?" I refuse to live in a "what if" world. Reality is hard enough to deal with on its own.

A young lady was driving and texting when she hit my truck that was parked on the side of the road. My truck is my livelihood. The funny thing is that I was not too concerned at the time about my truck. Did this young lady need medical attention? Was anybody else in the car who might need medical attention? Was everybody safe? I strongly felt that all material things like my truck could be replaced, but human life is what mattered most. I did suffer some minor inconveniences, and I don't choose to go through that again, but I came out with a bigger, more durable, less mileage, better truck than I had before. It was as if God was saying, *It is time for you to upgrade to a newer truck before this truck of yours breaks down.* For over a year now, when I get in my truck, I say, *Thank you, God, for this truck.* A blessing and a constant visual reminder to me of how great God is and how God has taken care of me all of my life.

Knowing me the way I do, I am surprised that I didn't take my totaled truck as just another disaster that happened to me.. It is just another negative brick in the wall of life, right? Now I feel like I am on my way to reprogramming my sub-conscious mind to find or even wait for what possible good that could come out of the situation I just went through. I do not believe that there is anybody in the world that does not experience some negative emotions or thoughts at some time or another. The "What ifs" are a big factor. What ifs are the match that starts the negative wildfire that can get out of control! Why is it so hard for us to realize that the "What ifs" do not control us? We are in control of the what ifs. For example: What if everything works out? What if this is for my good? What if I come out of this situation better than I was before?

I know what you are thinking: *You have to be kidding me. The "What ifs" never work out for good.* Let me ask you, do you want the "What ifs" to work to your advantage? Then believe that they can. It will not cost you anything, and you have nothing to lose, so why not see what happens? If the "What ifs" work out to your advantage one out of three times, then you are doing better than you were before. The trick is to remember that it is possible for the "What ifs" to be positive because it happened before.

Chapter Five

THERE IS A STORY

There is a story in the Gospels about a girl restored to life and a woman healed. Specifically, Matthew 9:18-26, Mark 5:21-43, and Luke 8:40-56. I wondered why the example of these two people healed (the woman and the girl) are tied together. The example of the power of Jesus that exists and the miracles that He was performing relates that a man named Jairus (a ruler of the synagogue) fell down before Jesus and begged him to come to his house and heal his daughter, who was dying. By this time, the miraculous healing powers of Jesus were well known, and everybody wanted to see and be around this Jesus. On the way, with the crowd pressing in on Him, I imagine to hear His every word and see what wonders Jesus might perform, there was a woman who had a flow of blood for twelve years. Nobody could heal her, and she spent all her livelihood on physicians to no avail. I also imagine that this woman, after so long of dealing with this problem, had tried every home remedy, talked to all the elder women who could advise her, and even went to the priest, who prayed over her. The bottom line is she was doomed to suffer with this ailment, and there was no possible way to be healed.

Then came this Jesus. When word spread to her that he was healing people of every type of ailment, I am sure a spring of hope rose up in her. *After all, the blind are seeing – and what about this woman Mary called Magdalene (Luke 8:2) who was healed of seven evil demons and other infirmities. If she could be healed, why couldn't I?* she surely thought to herself. No doubt this woman *knew* that she could be healed; there was no doubt. Her only problem was that she would have to press through the crowd and ask Jesus. *Oh why bother? I mean, could I really make it through all these people, and if I could, would Jesus actually grant my request to be healed? He is going to help this little girl; Jesus probably doesn't have time for me anyway*. This was going to be an uphill battle for anybody, even more so a sick woman.

I can imagine that she was thinking, *Maybe I won't even bother Jesus. After all, does Jesus have time for me? I am nobody. There are so many more important people than me around; just look at them all.* I am sure she pondered that, *Well, I'll just try to touch his garment and get out of there; that way I won't be bothering him. Jesus won't even know, and he can be on his way to help this young girl of Jairus, but I know that if I just touch him I will be healed and I can finally go on to a normal life. One thing is for sure: It's worth a shot.* So the battle continued to get through the crowd. The closer she got to Jesus the more she could feel her hope rising and her faith growing until finally she came up from behind Jesus and struggled to get her arm though all the people while still moving with the crowd – then that final reach. She did it; she touched Jesus.

The woman knew she'd touched Jesus because she immediately felt the flow of blood stop. Was she thinking *I am finally free from this ailment! It worked, my plan worked, I was right, I just needed to touch him.*

All of a sudden, Jesus said, "Somebody touched me, for I perceive power going out from me." (Luke 8:46) *Oh-oh I'm in trouble now. How did He know? I am the guilty one, and if Jesus knows power went out from Him, then He's going to know that it was me. I might as well fess up, maybe Jesus will go easy on me.*

The story goes that she came trembling and falling down before Him. She declared to Him in the presence of all the people the reason she had touched Him and how she was healed immediately. (Luke 8:47)

Then Jesus corrected her by saying, "Daughter, be of good cheer; your faith has made you well. Go in peace." (Luke 8:48) This woman realized it was not the act of touching Jesus that made her well, but that she had believed and her faith produced actions that caused her to touch Jesus that made her well.

About that time, someone came from the ruler of the synagogue's house, saying to him, "Your daughter is dead. Do not trouble the teacher." (Luke 8:49) I wonder what this woman who had the flow of blood thought. *Is it my fault? Was it because of my touching him that caused the delay? Was it my selfishness that caused this little girl to die?* Who would want to live with that kind of guilt? But when Jesus heard of the message, he answered by saying, "Do not be afraid, only believe, and she will be made well." (Luke 8:50) No doubt the woman might have thought, *That is what I did; I believed, and I was made well. Surely Jesus can make this little girl of Jairus well again.*

The story goes that when Jesus reached the home of Jairus, He said to the crowd that the girl was only sleeping. The people there ridiculed Him, but Jesus would not hear any of their negativity and even went so far as to put all of them out except for the mother and father of the child and Peter, James, and John. (Luke 8:51) I reasoned that if they let the negativity of the crowd influence them, then their disbelief would cause a negative reaction. The mother and father needed to believe, and why would Jesus continue to go there if there was no hope? The fact that Jesus still continued to travel to Jairus' home was testament that there was still hope. The crowd had to go because there is no believing when you are surrounded by negativity.

"Little girl, arise." (Luke 8:54) The little girl's spirit returned to her, and she arose immediately. (Luke 8:55) The story goes on to say that the little girl's parents were astonished. (Luke 8:56). The word "astonished" tells me that the parents must have been dealing with a certain amount of disbelief and every other emotion that comes with losing a child. Jesus' example of the power of believing is a lesson for us all. Peter, James and John witnessed this power of believing firsthand and used it throughout their ministry of Jesus, along with countless others.

Yet the story is not over. We must go back and figure out all the important extras that go along with it. For example, when the woman with the flow of blood touched Jesus to be healed, she was not denied access to the power that Jesus possessed. The power that Jesus possesses is free to all. Jesus will not deny anybody; they just need to believe this power is free for them. Not only is that shown here, but also in every healing miracle that Jesus and later His apostles exhibited. Not one person who believed that they could be healed in this time of Jesus was denied healing. All were granted access to this healing power for the glory and honor of God. Do you get it? We are all granted access to this power for the glory and honor of God, and the key to unlocking this power is believing. That is the secret I have been talking about: believing without allowing the negative baggage to stop us.

As to why this woman who was healed and a little girl restored to life are tied together is very important. The woman with the flow of blood shows us that we have access to the power of God, and the daughter of Jairus who could not believe for herself shows us that it is never too late, no matter what delay has taken place, and it is possible to believe for someone else. The little girl could not believe for herself since she had passed on. Others had to believe for her. We also know that with Jesus there are no such thing as impossibilities. These two people were healed specifically for the glory and honor of God and for us to see the key to life begins with believing.

Well, it just does not work that way nowadays. You are absolutely correct, but only because we have replaced believing in the glory and honor of God with believing in our own selfish desires. King David and Bathsheba had a baby (2 Samuel 12:15-23), but because of King David's sin the child was struck with illness. (How would you like to live with that?) King David pleaded with God, fasted, wept, and even slept on the ground for seven days. David's servants were terrified to come and tell him that the baby had passed on for fear of what his reaction would be. Would he harm himself? Would he harm them? When King David knew for sure that his baby had died, he got up, washed and anointed himself, and he ate. It was a total turnaround.

King David's servants could not understand. They knew the mental anguish that David had been going through; they'd witnessed it themselves, so why the big turnaround? The servants had to ask what was up.

"What is this that you have done? You fasted and wept for the child while he was alive, but when the child died, you arose and ate food." (2 Samuel 12:21) King David replied, "While the child was alive, I fasted and wept; for I said 'Who can tell whether the Lord will be gracious to me, that the child may live?'" (2 Samuel 12:22) David goes on to say, "But now he is dead; why should I fast? Can I bring him back again? I shall go to him, but he shall not return to me." (2 Samuel 12:22)

The astonishing thing is that King David did not question why or hold a grudge against God because the baby passed. David accepted God's decision and believed that he would go to the child. The love for his son did not end with death for the child and despair for him, but with an eternal love with no ending. David accepted with faith that there would be a future reunion with this child. The same faith that the woman with the flow of blood had that she would be made well. We all know that if you lose a child, it is devastating. I firmly believe that you cannot help but feel an insurmountable amount of pain, and it is okay to feel that pain. Let the pain run its course, but do whatever you can to remember that it is not over with, there is more to come with the loss of someone that you love or with some painful event. What I am saying is to think beyond the pain. Once there was a time when we had hope in what tomorrow will bring; now is the time to go back to that future.

Cathy was a cashier at a gas station. She was loved by everyone – just a good down-to-earth person. She would never do anybody any harm and was ready to help anyone who needed help. One day an ex-felon who was released from an Indiana prison and was on bail for attempted murder crossed the border into Illinois with two younger men. They went to the gas station where Cathy worked with the plan to rob it. They needed drug money. Cathy, who was filling in for a co-worker (who called off) freely gave the robber the $48 from the cash register. She was thinking about her four young children and her husband and didn't want any trouble.

One thing the robber learned in prison was that you never leave any witnesses, so he shot Cathy in the head. The scene was pretty gruesome. Cathy's brains were splattered all over the place. She died instantly.

Years later I had the chance to talk to Cathy's mother, Jane. This strong in faith Catholic lady was still crushed; her faith was gone. She would tell me, "Jimmy, why? Would God let this happen?" I would tell her God did not want this to happen. God was crushed by this man's actions and what he had done to Cathy too. All men have a thing called "free will," and it was his free will that took the life of Cathy. I told her it was time to forgive this man.

"Never," came the reply from Cathy's mother. "He took my little girl from me."

I said, "In Matthew 11:28, Jesus states, 'Come to me, all you who are weary and burdened, and I will give you rest.' Can it be that the "heavy laden" part is the baggage that we labor with that comes with unforgiveness? I thought that this man who killed Cathy was responsible for the hatred that was destroying Jane's soul. For years I talked with her, and I could see that when Cathy was killed, so was her mother. I had to somehow get her to understand that forgiveness was not only for the man who took her little girl's life, but also for her. Finally this mother said that she would have to think about what I was saying. Silently I thanked God. I felt like I'd had a breakthrough.

This hatred that she carried around with her was destroying her. Do the people who commit crimes realize how many people are affected by their actions? Cathy's kids, who grew up without their mother, suffered through tough times. I am a person who believes the unconditional love of a mother is a vital part of children as they grow. This unconditional love never leaves the child, and they pass that unconditional love on to their children. It is one of the cycles of life.

The guy who killed Cathy will spend the rest of his life in prison. He was sentenced to natural life and 20 years. *I wonder how much pain and agony his family has gone through?* Does he realize that his actions affected his family too? Did he have kids? What do they think? I began to wonder just how important is forgiveness anyway? Forgiveness must be pretty important because when Jesus taught us to pray, Jesus said in Matthew 6:12 that we should ask to be forgiven our debts, as we also have forgiven our debtors. This comes straight from the Lord's Prayer. The Lord's Prayer is a daily prayer or an example of a daily prayer, so it appears that the message that we are being taught is that it is important to forgive on a daily basis.

I believe that Jesus knew the importance of forgiveness. A sin, regardless if we are the sinner or someone who was sinned against, still carries with it that evil component that destroys us from the inside out. I am a perfect example. I admit and take responsibility for my actions. My sins have affected hundreds of people. Am I responsible for the unforgiveness that they might be continuing to carry around all this time? As for the people who have sinned against me, their sins affect me and them. Do they want my forgiveness for the contempt that I have held in my heart? Forgiveness for me was something that I needed for me. Holding anger and contempt in my heart stopped me from growing. When we forgive, we must remember that we do not have the power to pardon. Only God can pardon. Punishment is also on a spiritual level beyond our comprehension.

Romans 2:5 says, "But in accordance with your hardness and your impenitent heart, you are treasuring up for yourself wrath in the day of wrath and revelation of the righteous judgment of God." I believe this applies to an unforgiving heart as well as all our actions; after all, unforgiveness is an action that we are taking. I do understand that unforgiveness is extremely difficult to past, but it is possible.

I would go to Cathy's grave with her mother, we would pray and talk with her. Cathy would not want her mother to carry around hatred for this man who took her life, and it helped going there. Cathy's mother died in February 2018. I go to her grave and pray and talk to her. It helps me to do this. You see, Cathy's mother was my mother, and Cathy was my sister.

My sister Susie once told me what a blessing it was that God took Cathy. Susie understood that Cathy would have been just a body in a bed living on machines. It was hard for us both to thank God for Cathy passing on, *but now we both understand that God's grace and mercy surpasses our understanding,* and I would not have it any other way. We both believe that it is not over with yet; we will see Cathy again, and our love for our sister has not diminished one bit.

I understand the man who was convicted of killing my sister still maintains his innocence. I have no comment except to say that for me it was time for me to forgive and move on. I understand that any amount of unforgiveness would not add to his punishment, and the only person who was being hurt by my unforgiveness was me. The guilty person who killed my sister might not even care if I forgive him. My forgiveness does not pardon him for the wrong that he has done; it just brings me to a state of acceptance that I cannot change the fact that my sister is gone, and I must go to her – which I am sure I will.

One of the most meaningful stories of the Bible comes from John 8:3-11, (3) "Then the scribes and Pharisees brought to Him a woman caught in adultery. And when they had set her in the midst, (4) they said to Him, "Teacher, this woman was caught in adultery, in the very act. (5) Now Moses, in the law, commanded us that such should be stoned. But what do you say?"

What the Bible doesn't say is that you have to imagine. There is a crowd of people bringing a guilty woman to Jesus – why? The crowd's mindset is to test Jesus. Their minds is already made up. They are sure, they are confident, and they know that this woman is supposed to be stoned. Anything that is said not in agreement would surely start an argument. Jesus knows what the crowd is up to, and Jesus also knows that this is a big opportunity to show that this is a part of "The Turning Point" from the old covenant (Moses law equals stoning) to the new covenant (grace and mercy).

So Jesus stoops down and writes on the ground with His finger. Well that's unusual – why is Jesus stalling? But Jesus is not stalling. At this time Jesus is now extending grace to the crowd. Jesus knows that he must break their mindset. At this time the crowd has no choice but to think, *Why is this man Jesus doing this? Didn't he hear us? He must not know what to say.* That was enough. The whole crowds' attention was no longer on the woman; it was on Him.

Jesus says to them John 8:7 …"He who is without sin among you, let him throw a stone at her first." After which Jesus stoops back down and continues to write in the dirt. Another extension of grace. This is their time to ponder His answer. Naturally the crowd is no longer concerned about the guilty woman because they are contemplating their own sins. One by one, they begin to quietly leave, their own conscience and the heaviness of their souls condemning them. Isn't it ironic that what is condemning them is what began as a judging lynch mob?

The big question is after all of this woman's accusers left is why didn't the woman leave? When a guilty person is caught, the natural usual response is to run. Especially when the punishment is to be stoned. This woman was still guilty of adultery, and the punishment still stood in effect. Did she sense that because Jesus just saved her from a stoning she should wait to hear what he had to say? This was a whole new concept and totally against the old law.

Could it be that the woman intuitively sensed a change? After all, women were not considered to be the equal of men. Otherwise the crowd would have brought the woman and the man, who was also guilty of adultery, to Jesus at this time. The man got off free from the beginning or had to deal with the punishment that was set forth in place at the time. This may be why the crowd was so bold in their actions. (We do not know if there were any women in the crowd, probably so.)

John 8:10 "When Jesus had raised Himself up and saw no one but the woman, He said to her, 'Woman, where are those accusers of yours? Has no one condemned you?' (11) She said, 'No one, Lord.' And Jesus said to her, 'Neither do I condemn you; go and sin no more.'" WOW! Talk about grace and mercy. This woman went from the stone pit to forgiveness. This is the turning point.

The question is are you the type of person who would be a part of the lynch mob, or are you the type of person to side with Jesus? Everybody I know is guilty of something and probably deserving of a stoning. Imagine you are now in that woman's sandals – how would you feel about Jesus? Is it not true that every one of us can fit in that woman's sandals in real life? After all, she was guilty of something, and aren't we all guilty of something? It is also true that Jesus got us all out of a stoning, at least all who are guilty of something and do their part and believe.

Since Jesus doesn't condemn sinners, why should I? Why should you? The smart thing for me to do is remember what Jesus told this woman in verse 11: "Go and sin no more." I'll let Jesus do the judging; after all, He's better at it than I am. Is there a turning point in your life? I go back and restate that it is my job to treat all people with dignity, honor and respect. My judging someone does not affect them one bit, and why should they care? I have no problem judging the situation or the surrounding environment that I find myself in. It is easy for me to walk into some place and say to myself, *This probably is not the place that is best for my going in a forward progressive motion.* If someone judges me or has something bad to say about me, don't even tell me. I don't need to know I cannot please everybody in the world. I can only do my best.

Chapter Six

MOST IMPORTANT

I am a selfish person! Well, that just sounds like a self-important, conceited statement. Yet I humbly say this is a true statement. I know what you are thinking: *Why would you make a statement like that?* Because it is most important. Don't misunderstand; it is not that my goal is to keep my stuff for me, or no one else matters except for my satisfaction and if one of us has to die, well I hope you had a good life. No; I am a selfish person because I know that in order for me to love you, I must be able to love me first. That was not an easy task for me. I have a past full of mistakes and wrong decisions; as a matter of fact, I would say that no one in this great big old earth has made more mistakes than me. Okay, that is probably an over-statement, but I am sure I am in the running for making my share of mistakes.

It is amazing to me how God works. How could God take a broken-down man like me with all these terrible mistakes in his past and jumble them all together, toss them around with some incredible miracle working power and come up with the end result of me. A totally humble, extremely grateful, happy man? I am still a work in progress, but I know with the power of God this is just the beginning. I love the man that God has made me to be, and I will do my best to further the good part of me. I don't like my past mistakes, but I know I can dwell on those past mistakes or I can choose to move forward and dwell on my future successes – which are many. I don't even know what they are yet, but I believe that they are.

An important thing in life to remember is that we all go through hardship. Even those who seem to be extremely blessed in this life have had to go through some kind of drama that set them back. It is their gratitude and positive outlook that lets them know it is not over with. Life is a series of emotional hills and valleys. Some hills seem like mountains that we must struggle to go up, but with faith and believing that we can, we can move those mountains out of our way. Jesus said in Mathew 17:20, "Because of your unbelief; for assuredly, I say to you, if you have faith as a mustard seed you will say to this mountain, 'move from here to there,' and it will move; and nothing will be impossible for you."

It is amazing to me that such a minimal amount of faith can tie us into this huge amount of power when we put this faith into action. Naturally, having this kind of faith does not come easy. We are programmed from an early age, and for some reason it is so easy for us to believe the negative and so hard for us to believe the positive. The question is how do we change over to a higher self-esteem which we are worthy to tap into the power that comes with being more positive and having more faith?

I am sure one way is to be more helpful to the people around us. When our lives are not centered on us and what *is in it for me?* attitude, we lay a foundation of love on which to build the rest of our lives. Many times in my life I have felt like I have been taken advantage of. A prime example of this is a time when I was working. You have to understand that when I work I work for the glory and honor of God, so the person I am working for is getting a really good deal. One day while working, my co-worker was told to help me, and they said, "I'll just let Jim do all the work, and I can stand here and get paid." For the most part that is what they did.

Now I will admit that it takes a lot of guts to make a statement like that to the boss. I know I don't have that much nerve. I will also admit that when my boss told me that statement, I was pretty upset. This person was definitely taking advantage of me. After thinking about it I had to come to terms with the fact that I'd agreed to work for a certain wage, and I got paid for the work that I did. Actually I was paid more because the job took longer to be completed since I was mostly on my own. Another thing is I did not specify to the boss that his other workers must work the same as me. So I had no complaint there. Also I understand that not everybody works for the glory and honor of God like I do, so I have no right to expect them to work as I do. In the end I realized that I had no regrets. My actions held true to my belief that God will reward me for my intentions. Working for the glory and honor of God, I humbly expect God to take notice and reward me accordingly. Which God already has a million times over!

There is a saying that if you tell a lie enough times, you will actually believe your own lie. I love this statement and cannot figure out why we don't use it to our advantage. I do not understand how our brain works in such a way that we will believe our own lie, but I do know if I tell myself something like *I am a happy person* or *I believe all things happen for good to those who love God and are called according to His purpose, and I love God* enough times eventually my brain will believe it, and I will take on the necessary characteristics that will make my life more enjoyable. Furthermore, through faith and believing I too can call into existence things which do not exist as though they did exist. Abraham, by believing that he would be the father of many nations even though he and Sarah were beyond children bearing years, was the father of many nations. Abraham did not consider his own body since he was about one hundred years old, but he believed, and that was accredited to him for righteousness. In essence, Abraham believed and would not allow the negativity to come in. This is our goal: to not let the negativity in.

The first thing that we should be telling ourselves is *It is a fact that I am a happy person, I am a happy person now, and I am completely capable of being a happy person no matter what happens, and no matter who says what about me, and no one is holding me back from being happy.* I know what you are thinking: *Oh sure, I tried your theory for two weeks and I am still miserable.* Well, sorry, and I am surprised your dedication to make your life more positive and happy only extended for two weeks. How many years were dedicated to living the way you don't want? Why should your metamorphosis or your new birth to a new life only take two weeks to change? Plus the more serious you are, the faster the change will take place. Also did you surround yourself with positive reinforcement? *Congratulations! I did it I am a new person – a happy, positive person.* Are you hanging out with your old depressing friends who validate by their existence that life is full of nothing but struggles, and then you die? My point is that you cannot live the same life doing the same thing with the same people who are content with where they are. Surrounding ourselves with a more positive type of person who has dreams and goals will enhance our chances of breaking free of the old lifestyle that we have lived for far too long. Change does not come instantaneously; change in this case is a lifestyle.

There is a Scripture in the Bible that states, "Therefore I say to you, whatever things you ask when you pray, believe that you receive them, and you will have them." (Mark 11:24) This verse is not telling us to believe our own lie. It is telling us to believe with expectancy. Also it doesn't say that we should just ask once, but that we should keep asking until we receive what we are asking for. I believe the repeating of our asking is not to finally get God to grant our request because God is tired of hearing us, but for us to finally believe without doubt we can get what we are asking for. There is no doubt in my mind that the woman with the flow of blood who touched Jesus told herself many times, *I know that I can be healed*, even though she tried everything and failed. With twelve years of failing behind her, there had to be some doubt that would have crept in her mind that would have caused her to think, *What if this doesn't work?*

It is very interesting that believing can work two ways. One way believing can work is with faith; the other is with doubt. It appears that the easier of the two is the negative doubt way; only with repeating the believing with faith can we get our brain and our heart to accept this new way of believing. The new way of believing takes time and energy. If you want to receive what you are asking for, then you have to believe. You have to believe without doubt, without fear, and without the negative baggage of your past. This is definitely an uphill battle for most of us, whose lives are not filled with all the glorious, good things in life. Not all of us had a silver spoon, where everything was handed to us and our lives have not had a lot of drama, but I have come to find out the things that we worked for and earned in this life are the things that mean the most to us.

Believing with expectancy opens us up to God and the powers that created the universe, and I am sure without a doubt that the true nature of God will give us all that we ask for. Especially when we ask for things that will bring glory and honor to God. After all, how can you not give thanks to the one who has answered all your prayers? Every day of my life the people I know and the people I meet know how grateful I am for the blessings that I have received and the blessings I have not yet received (I believe that they are coming). Can you imagine that you are blessed every day of your life and not just the occasional unexpected blessing? Well, you are, and it is a lot easier to see the blessings when you get rid of all the negativity or shake off the negative emotions, like when the guy cut you off in traffic and the countless times when you feel that you were wronged.

If you are like me, you will make the choice to be a more positive person, but the negative thoughts will not go away. It takes time and dedication to your own life to make a difference to you. To clear out all the past baggage that will force doubt into your thinking. Let us face it; we have been living our whole life with this preconceived notion that we don't deserve all the things that we really do deserve.

Let us say that you are married, do you rely on your spouse for your happiness and when your spouse does not live up to your expectation, it's their fault that you are not happy? Did your marriage vows specifically say, "I do, but only if every day of my life you are in charge of making me happy?" Although it is my heart's desire for my spouse to be happy, I realize I am not in charge of her happiness, and there will be times when happiness just will not be there – her fault, my fault, there is no blame to place on either of us. If my spouse is not happy do I have to be unhappy too? Well, if I am tied into the power of Jesus, I will be happy. Also I will be concerned for her unhappiness and hope that she will be concerned for my unhappiness, and I am sure we will do our best to help solve any problems that arise, but I will not lay my happiness on my spouse and make it her responsibility that I be happy. Everyone is in charge of their own happiness.

When I am at work do I grumble every time a problem arises? No; I can guarantee you on every job there will be some problems. A co-worker, a machine breaks down, the boss, and a million other possibilities. There is no law that states we have to be upset. Let your co-worker be upset. The machine will be fixed or replaced and the boss will be the boss. Since I know not everything will work out perfectly, then it is up to me to choose to stay in that peaceful mood and not allow anybody to steal my joy from me. *Oh sure, if it were only that easy, never to get mad or upset.* I can hear you telling me, *Well, you are not around the people that I am around, and these people can easily rub me the wrong way.* Yes, I agree people can rub me the wrong way too (far too often I admit).

I have been around people that have rubbed me the wrong way so many times that I literally thought that I would love to rip out my eyes so I don't have to look at them any longer. I just couldn't understand why someone would give up on their own life and continue in their miserable ways and want you to be miserable with them. It is almost as if they have resigned themselves to be a victim because that is where they feel most comfortable or they fear that it could be worse or they just need attention, and they cannot get it anywhere else. Plus some people are just mean because they can be, which doesn't make sense to me either.

One day I found myself praying *Lord, I just cannot take this person any longer. What do You want me to do?* Deep down inside I heard the words, "Be patient." *Well, that is not what I wanted to hear. I have shown love, I have been patient, I have been kind, I have been supportive, I have gone above and beyond the call of duty to do everything I possibly can to be a positive influence for Your glory and honor.* Then I heard deep down inside, "What a coincidence. I have done all of those things for you and have shown you grace and mercy over the past fifty-eight years, and you are not perfect. Should I give up on you?" *Well, Lord... since you put it that way.*

It is easy to get mad and angry at people, and no one should deny those emotions. Let them run their course, but it is truly up to us how long we stay mad and angry. Plus some people are just dangerous, and I in no way say stick around them. It doesn't make sense to stay in a dangerous situation no matter how much you pray for God to fix it. If you feel like you are stuck in a relationship and you cannot leave because you have nowhere to go and there are kids to think about too, then at that particular moment you are lacking the faith that God will take care of you. A separation might help everyone involved to get their mind together, and most importantly, we are all responsible to take care of ourselves, which includes our mental well-being. Even Jesus would go up on a mountain to pray (see Mark 6:46 – Luke 5:16). I imagine that even Jesus needed to decompress, to get his thoughts together, and to rejuvenate with having to deal with all these people who went astray from the truth.

Chapter Seven

COMPLAINING

I always found it fascinating that in the Bible, when people did complain against God, it did not end up well for them.

"[B]earing with one another, and forgiving one another, if anyone has a complaint against another; even as Christ forgave you, so you also must do." (Colossians 3:13)

"Do all things without complaining and disputing." (Philippians 2:14)

"... nor complain, as some of them also complained, and were destroyed by the destroyer." (1 Corinthian 10:10)

I am all for venting my feelings to someone I trust when I get overwhelmed with life, but I am not for complaining. It is so easy to complain about everything, yet I am learning that complaining does not do us any good. By the grace of God I am an extremely blessed person. We have campfires in the backyard, we look up at the stars, listen to our favorite music and roast hot dogs, sausages, and s'mores, and we talk. I can get so lost in the peacefulness of God's heavenly beauty that it just about brings me to tears. The people who know me and know what I have gone through in my life can see the gratitude on my face. They know that this peaceful setting is so far out of my imagination and that I am in awe that I am even alive, let alone blessed enough to be a part of such a wonderful life. I have no choice, and I humbly say that I need to face the fact that since I have given myself one hundred percent to Jesus, my life is a testament to others. You may think, *Big deal, you had a campfire. That is not really my thing.*

Well, I say, what is your thing? What is that thing that you like to do so much that it puts you in such a peaceful state that you feel like the power of the universe is right there for you to reach out and get a hold of? What is that thing in life that rejuvenates you to keep going and all of a sudden you want to be a better person? Do it! Do whatever it takes to find that spiritual oneness with your creator, and do it correctly. Because nothing brings you more joy, more love, more abundance of whatever you need like gratitude. Being grateful is a positive state of mind; it is like a key to the power of God when you can say *Thank you, God, for my life.*

Whereas complaining is a negative state of mind, let me remind you what the Bible says: "nor complain, as some of them also complained, and were destroyed by the destroyer." (1 Corinthian 10:10) Complaining is a tool used by the destroyer against us. Who is the destroyer, anyway? We have to go back to the book of Exodus to find out who the destroyer is. In the book of Exodus, it tells us the story of Moses leading the Hebrews out of Egypt. There was a Passover instituted, representing deliverance and new beginnings. A sacrificed lamb's blood was placed on the doorpost and lintel. If you did this act of faith, then the Lord would pass over and not allow the destroyer to come into your house and strike you.

We don't need to put lambs' blood on our doorways now; besides that, back then the act of putting the lambs' blood on the door frame signified a faith, trust, hope and belief in God. We can do that in a number of ways to show that we believe in the ultimate sacrifice of Jesus as our lambs' blood. Now if you want to keep away from the destroyer, then disable one of the destroyer's best used tools: negative thinking. How do you do that? "Concerning the works of men, *by the word of your lips*, I have kept away from the path of the destroyer." (Psalms 17:4) So we can see that King David concentrated on God's promises and would not allow negative thinking to bring him down. When David was on his game, he was very confident in his belief in God. Complaining opens up the power of the destroyer, and once the destroyer gets his foot in the door, it is game on, buddy.

We can learn a lot from the Hebrews in the Old Testament. For four hundred and fifty years they were held in captivity as slaves to the Egyptians. It stands to reason that during those four hundred and fifty years they picked up some pretty bad thinking habits and probably a custom or two from the Egyptians that went against their original beliefs. There were actual times after they were freed from the Egyptians that they complained so much that in their thinking it would have been better to go back and be slaves to the Egyptians. Can you imagine that? You have a choice to go into the promised land that you are entitled to and worthy of or go back to being a slave, and your choice is to go back to being a slave.

Well, you have that choice now. You can choose to be happy, positive, worthy, full of love and energy, and tied into the power of God, or you can choose to live a life of just getting by and *I hope nothing bad happens* or *I have done so many bad things in my life and I am unworthy of the good things in life*. What is it going to be? I know what you are thinking: *Well, it is not just as simple as that*. I agree!

It took forty years for the Hebrews to make an eleven-day trip from slavery to the Promised Land. They were so full of misconceptions and doubt that they spent way too much time complaining instead of believing in the promises that God would provide for them what they were worthy of that none of them made it into the Promised Land. Except for the two men who held on to their belief, hope and expectation that God would provide. Caleb and Jacob had the perception that the glass was half full; the rest of the Hebrews had the perception that the glass was half empty. Caleb and Jacob thrived in the desert while all the others died there. Technically there was the same amount of liquid in the glass. Are you going to be grateful for having enough liquid to get you to the next glass of refreshment, or are you going to complain that you want more now?

It appears to me that with all the negative events that are going on in the world now, way too many people have the perception that the glass is half empty. With that kind of attitude like the Hebrews, I don't see them entering the Promised Land, and unfortunately their glass will remain half empty. They will always see the setbacks of life as a sign of their unworthiness and will remain in the "just get by" mentality. The destroyer, the punisher, the accuser, whatever you want to call it, has its firm grip on the world's mental state. Like Eve in the Garden of Eden, people are choosing to be swayed by the great lie. "Then the serpent said to the woman, 'You will not surely die. 5 For God knows that in the day you eat of it your eyes will be opened, and you will be like God, knowing good and evil.'" (Genesis 3:4, 5)

We are now like God in the sense that we know good and evil. Thank God that this event took place. This event was the steppingstone that launched all people into a new dimension of life. Think about it: We through our own creative ability can choose to have the life that we want. With courage and faith we trek forward in the direction that we want to go. Every setback or negative event, with great expectation in the powers that be, can now be seen as a positive steppingstone to a greater life, a more worthy and deserving life.

You hear all the time that God is everywhere. So is his power, and that power is free for our use. Understand that with great power comes great responsibility. Abuse the power and don't be surprised if your abuse is what you are calling back into your own life. Just like Adam and Eve in the garden, your eyes are now opened and you understand good and evil. Abuse of power brings in the negative. If you do not believe in God at all, I can guarantee if you choose to live a positive life, your life will be more positive. If you choose to live a faith-filled positive life, your possibilities are endless.

Chapter Eight

GUILT

How long do I need to feel guilty when I do something wrong? Days, months, years – or maybe I should feel guilty my whole lifetime. Guilt is a negative but very useful emotion. It keeps us on track; if we feel guilt we are off track. If we remember that guilt is a tool to be used to get through life, then it has its advantages. If we just keep our guilt tool with us at all times because that is the way we were raised or that is what our church promotes, I am telling you now it is time to put down that tool and give it a rest until needed.

I am a very faith-filled man. I believe what the word of God tells me, and I do a lot of research on everything that comes up in my life that I don't understand. The word of God to me is a sort of instructional manual to help me get through the trying times especially. When I do something wrong and guilt hits me, I have found that it is more advantageous for me to run to God with this guilt rather than run away and let the feelings of unworthiness take over. 1 John 1:9 states that "If we confess our sins, He is faithful and just to forgive us our sins and to cleanse us from all unrighteousness." And it also states in Psalms 103:12, "As far as the east is from the west, So far has He removed our transgressions from us." Since this is true, why must I feel guilt for so long after I am forgiven?

The verses that I just stated have a great deal of power attached to them. They teach us that when we know that we have done something wrong and our conscience is bothering us, it is because our actions have condemned us. Not only that, but we have put ourselves in a position where we have fallen out of God's good graces, and the negativity that accompanies our demise can easily spread like wildfire. We can sit there the rest of our lives feeling condemned, or we can take action. We already know that we must stay away from the activity that caused the guilt in the first place, and if we are remorseful, then we will. Yet we are not done. We still must confess our wrongful activities to God in order to put the guilt tool down. Thankfully God is all about love, mercy and grace, and it is in God's character to forgive us. God will remove that transgression as far as the east is from the west. These verses do not say that God will think about it and get back to us at a later date about the forgiveness that you desire. Forgiveness occurs instantly. These verses don't say that you have used up all your chances and you are on your own now; these verses don't say that you will escape punishment from your negative deed. These verses say *I have forgiven you and will remember no more.* If God can forgive you, then in order to forgive ourselves we must put that guilt tool down and move forward. That will show that we are remorseful. This usually entails making right the wrong that occurred, if that is possible. It is not in our best interest to condemn ourselves for long periods of time by carrying around this guilt. God has forgiven you, so let it go.

Don't be surprised if you by chance hurt someone emotionally or physically that their forgiveness doesn't come as immediate as God's forgiveness. You will definitely have to prove you are sorry and earn their trust, and some forgiveness will never come. Society is by nature very unforgiving, and society believes that people don't change. I have heard it said that a leopard can't change its spots. Meaning like animals, people don't change. Well, society is incorrect. People do have the ability to change. What puts us above animals is our ability to change. Besides that, I am not a leopard or a turtle or a frog or a gazelle; I am a human being, and I can create the life that I want.

Let us learn from King David. It was only when King David let down his guard that he allowed the destroyer to creep in and knock him on his behind. After being knocked down and realizing that he was knocked down, King David did whatever it took to get back into God's good graces along with the power that comes with belief. "Create in me a clean heart, O God, and renew a steadfast spirit within me." (Psalms 51:10) When someone makes a statement like this one, it is because they are guilt-ridden about some action that they did in their life, and negativity is filling their head. I personally am very grateful for the Psalms. They show just how human King David was. His example shows how we can be human and make mistakes, realize what those mistakes are, take responsibility for those mistakes, and then move on without the guilt-ridden suitcase that most of us carry around.

We need to follow King David's example to do whatever it takes to get back into God's good graces, and then we can move on. You and I can do the right thing in life when we are not carrying around a suitcase of past guilt. When I feel good about me, I can conquer the world, and I find myself helping people that I normally would not even pay attention to. When I feel guilt, my self-esteem is so low I cannot even help myself. I just feel so unworthy, my health is not good, and I really pay in my sub-conscious mind. It is better for me to avoid doing things that make me feel guilt. By the way, King David went on to do many wonderful things in his life. He was a man after God's own heart.

I was talking the other day with a friend, and we were going over how guilt can destroy a person. How easy it would be to feel guilt, run to God for forgiveness, and then go right back and do the same thing that you felt guilt for in the first place. If this happens, then you don't really feel remorseful about the wrong that occurred in the first place. The forgiveness you thought that you had is a figment of your imagination. Meaning that the negative cycle that you are stuck in will be that much harder to get out of. You should not expect to receive access to the power that is free for the taking from God. As a matter of fact, if you keep committing the same wrong over and over again, that would seem like you are just trying to get away with something, and you are playing a game to see if you can win, but you've created a negative block which will hinder you from going forward. Obviously, when you are sorry, you make amends to be forgiven for the act that brought on the guilt, and you stay away from the deed that brought on the guilt in the first place.

We must also remember that being forgiven does not mean that we escape punishment that would be a pardon. When you ask for forgiveness, what you are saying is that you take responsibility for your actions, and you accept the punishment no matter what it is, because most importantly you find it absolutely necessary to get back into God's good graces like King David did in Psalms 51. This way you can put down the guilt for the glory and honor of God. With the guilt, it is too heavy to give God glory and move forward. Your mind is not on going forward; it is on how heavy the load you are carrying is. I would much rather ask for forgiveness, receive forgiveness, make amends, put down that guilt tool, and move in a forward progressive motion where I am confident that I can reach out and grab hold of the free power provided by God's lovingkindness. This act itself brings God glory and honor.

There are some wrongful acts that bring on this feeling of guilt that are against God alone. Nobody was hurt physically or emotionally, and nobody even knows that you did this deed that is bringing on this feeling of guilt, but you know that this act is stopping you from going in a forward progressive motion. It is stopping you from reaching your full potential, and it brings on feelings of being unworthy. Maybe it is an addiction that is well-hidden, or it is something else that only you and your creator know about. There is just something there that deep down inside you know is wrong, and you don't know how to fix it because you tried and tried and you are tired of the guilt and you are tired of being held back by your own actions when you know you can go farther.

There is a particular story in the Bible about a demon-possessed man in the Gospel of Luke. The story is told about how Jesus and his disciples traveled by boat to the country of the Gadarenes. When Jesus stepped out of the boat onto the land, there was this man from the city who had demons for a long time.

The story goes that he wore no clothes, nor did he live in a house, but in the tombs. When he saw Jesus, he cried out, fell down before Him, and with a loud voice said, "What have I to do with You, Jesus, Son of the Most High God? I beg you, do not torment me!" For Jesus had commanded the unclean spirit to come out of the man. Because the demons had often seized him, this man was so dangerous to himself and to other people that they kept him under guard, bound with chains and shackles; and he broke the bonds and was driven by the demon into the wilderness.

Jesus asked him, saying, "What is your name?" And he said, "Legion," because many demons had entered him. *The demons begged Him that He would not command them to go out into the abyss.* A short distance away, a herd of many swine was feeding there on the mountain. So they begged Him that He would permit them to enter them. *Jesus granted their request.* Then the demons went out of the man and entered the swine, and the herd ran violently down the steep place into the lake and drowned.

When those who fed them saw what had happened, they fled and told it in the city and in the country. Then they went out to see what had happened, and came to Jesus, and found the man from whom the demons had departed, sitting at the feet of Jesus, clothed and in his right mind. And they were afraid. They also who had seen it told them by what means he who had been demon-possessed was healed.

This story is very important to us all. First it shows how Jesus traveled to the man who was demon possessed – the man did not reach out to him, but the demons did through the man. Second, we see that this man did plenty of bad things in his life, so much so that the authorities actually had to keep him bound with chains and shackles. I would imagine this man would have plenty to feel guilty about, and I am sure that his emotional state was one of unworthiness. Nowadays we have prisons that promote unworthiness, guilt and shame with no expectations upon the prisoners except to come back to prison once they are released. Third, we see that even the worst, the demons, only had to ask for grace and mercy to receive grace and mercy. Most importantly, the characteristic of God is to unconditionally give grace and mercy. Do you understand that Jesus extended grace and mercy to the demons all because they asked? How much more will God extend grace and mercy to you and me when we ask for it? I believe that Jesus comes to us every day in some fashion ready to give us unconditional grace and mercy. Jesus does not say, "Okay, I'll do this for you, but you have to do something for me." No; Jesus extends grace and mercy, and it is our decision as to whether or not we want to stay connected to the one who can keep us whole or return to the ways that got us in this bad place in the beginning.

Fourth, we see that there is still a consequence; the demons went into the swine, and the swine "ran violently down the steep place into the lake and drowned." That word *violently* conjures up images in my mind of a crazy stampede. The people who saw what happened actually got scared and took off so they could tell others about what happened. The power that Jesus used to free the man from the demons is extraordinary and shows that Jesus has complete control over the demons. What were the tools that Jesus used? Grace and mercy.

The story goes on to say that the Gadarenes saw this demon-possessed man sitting at Jesus' feet in his right mind, and they were afraid. I often wonder why they were afraid. You would think that the Gadarenes would have been grateful for taking care of this problem with the man, but instead they were more concerned with the pigs that they had lost. Maybe it is because they had their own secret demons that they were embarrassed about and did not want those demons brought to light. Whatever the case, the Gadarenes asked Jesus to depart because they were seized with fear. Jesus did leave, but not before denying the request of the once demon-possessed man to come with Jesus. Jesus knew that this man would bring more glory and honor to God if he stayed and related to others what God had already did for him. For informational purposes, the man did as Jesus requested throughout the whole city. His decision was to stay tied into the power that set him free, and I am sure he went on to have a great life.

We all have secrets, we all have embarrassments, and we all have reason to feel guilty and unworthy. I thank God for these acts because I know that I cannot grow without these stepping-stones in my way. I understand that I grow during the trying character-building times in my life, and once I do grab ahold of the power that will help me to beat my downfall, I will be a better and stronger person. I am closer to being the man that I am supposed to be. I am a work in progress, and as long as I keep trying to go forward, I will go forward. I will not allow myself to get in the way of my growth. I am worthy, and I know that with the power of God I can beat anything that brings on this emotion of guilt because that is what I am supposed to do.

Chapter Nine

THE SECRET TO IT ALL

I told you that I know the secret, and I even told you the secret to life is believing. So we all understand that the secret to life is to believe the impossible, and to believe the impossible is possible. We can also see that believing is not as easy as it seems; we let too much negativity get in the way. Our parents lay guilt trips on us when something wrong happens, our churches promote guilt and fear if we commit a wrong, and make us feel like we are unworthy and we condemn ourselves because we know that we are guilty of something. I don't understand why we are not taught to get past the guilt by anybody. If we are forgiven the moment we ask God for forgiveness, then why must we feel guilt for days, weeks months or even years after? The people around us complain, and they are convinced that life is nothing but one miserable disaster after another. There is a mountain of negativity that we must battle through. My question is why isn't anybody showing us the way to move that mountain out of the way so we can use the positive power that is free for us to use?

God is showing how to move the mountain. "For assuredly, I say to you, whoever says to this mountain, 'Be removed and be cast into the sea,' and does not doubt in his heart, *but believes that those things he says will be done*, he will have whatever he says." (Matthew 11:23) I revert back to a story that was first published in the 1930s. It was written by Watty Piper, and the book was called "The Little Engine That Could.[2]" If we want to move this mountain of negativity and cast it into the sea, we definitely need to keep telling ourselves *I think I can, I think I can* until we are convinced that we actually can, just as that little train did in

---

2 Watty Piper, The Little Engine that Could

the story, then it will be so. Our higher power is telling us that it is so, so it must be.

Interestingly, we are born with such power in us that we can create the life that we always wanted. It is never too late to start, and it is something we will never finish. "Death and life are in the power of the tongue, and those who love it will eat its fruit." (Proverbs 18:21) In life we use many tools. There are hand tools, garden tools, kitchen tools, and every kind of tool that you can imagine, but the most important tool that you will ever use every day of your life is a power tool called the tongue. Whatever job you work at, there should be a sign that reminds you to use safety first. With this power tool that we are born with, extra caution should be taken. The tongue can cause death when used incorrectly, and it can also cause you pain and misery that you have to live with for the rest of your life.

When used correctly, the tongue power tool can bring you love, joy, comfort, happiness, gratitude, satisfaction, and a whole slew of positive feelings beyond your wildest imagination. Like with all tools, we have a choice as to how we use it. For example, when a loved one is hurting, we tend to speak words of comfort to them because we want them to stop hurting. That is a correct way to use your power tool called the tongue. The amazing thing is for most people it is easier to speak words of comfort to others than to speak words of comfort to ourselves. It is easier to believe negative things about our own lives than to tell ourselves *Don't worry, it will be okay.* I am the same way. I was raised to be a tough love kind of person, especially when it comes to my inner child. I want everyone to experience the love that God has for them, and I believe that you will not experience Gods precious love by choosing to use your power tool incorrectly.

Matthew 12:37 states, "For by your words you will be justified, and by your words you will be condemned." This verse is very concerning because it squarely puts the responsibility of justification and condemnation on each one of us. In essence we can say whether we have a good life or bad life is solely our responsibility. Not only that, but it is our own words that can cause what type of life we have. "A man will be satisfied with good by the fruit of his mouth, and the recompense of a man's hands will be rendered to him." (Proverbs 12:14)

I know what you are thinking: *Well, this happened to me and that happened to me way back when, and it's just been one thing after another.* I am sorry that you have gone through some bad things in your life. You are not alone; all people go through bad things in their life, and I personally cannot imagine the pain that you might be feeling. There comes a time in our life when we have to choose how long we are going to be a victim. Are we going to let the past or what is happening to us now ruin the future that could be more than we can imagine? There is a Scripture in the Bible that clearly states "Either make the tree good and its fruit good, or else make the tree bad or its fruit bad; for a tree is known by its fruit." (Matthew 12:33) This is where you can use your power tool – the tongue – to your advantage. Proceed with caution; remember, safety first. Use your power tool to your advantage. Say these affirmations out loud: *I am not going to allow the past to ruin my future. I choose not to be a victim. I will do whatever it takes to get past the past. I will do whatever it takes to get past the addiction. I am moving on.*

Believe what you say, and it will happen. In the beginning, doubt will creep in, and you may say *Aw, this will never work. I can tell myself these things a million times, and I'll still be the same.* The reprogramming of your subconscious mind takes time. It has had plenty of time to believe the negative, and the subconscious mind is stubborn. It will want to keep you as you always were, what it is used to. We are training our subconscious mind to have a fresh new look at things, a positive approach so when we are going through the tough spots in life it will automatically find the positive. I want my mind to automatically come up with what is positive in a bad situation because coming up with the negative just has not worked for me.

I admit some of us are buried a little bit deeper than others when it comes to our past, our drug addictions, our alcoholism, our anxiety, depression, and the million other things that can keep us from reaching our goal of happiness and living without the addiction and the fear of regressing back to our past. The fact of the matter is that we are all creators of our own lives, and the sad truth is that the life we are living may not be the life we want to live, but it is the life we are choosing to live. We are responsible for how we live. Sadly, that means that we are responsible, and we cannot point our fingers outward. In order to move on, we have to point our fingers inward and take the necessary steps to move in a forward progressive motion.

I know what you are thinking: *I am not choosing to live this way! Why would anybody choose to live this way?* I agree with you: Why would anybody choose to live this way? Maybe because they fear it could be worse, or maybe they are afraid, or maybe they have religious beliefs that will not allow them to move on, or maybe they just don't know how to move on. There could be an unimaginable amount of reasons why we live in a way that we are not choosing. I do have one question though: If you are living in a way that is not what you want, what have you done *that has worked* to change your life to make it what you want it to be? I say that because we have might have tried a million things, but nothing has worked. Well, try believing, and don't give up in one week or two weeks. Try for the rest of your life.

Be warned: To have the life that you want is not a snap your fingers and poof you are now happy with the most perfect life. No; the metamorphosis that we are talking about is a journey. There will be many times you'll fall on your face, and there is a mountain of discouragement to move out of the way. There comes a time in your life where you have to ask yourself, *How bad do I want it?* It is almost as if the evil forces in life do not want to let you go, and they know the right buttons to push to make you fail and to stop you from the most important thing in the universe that we all need to do – to believe you can succeed. I live my life by this saying: "All things happen for good to those who love God and are called according to his purpose." (Romans 8:28) So even my failures today will be for good. I don't need to understand what the good is because I know God can turn my failures around for his glory. Some good will come out of it. Not only do I know this, but I believe it! *The power that God has placed in the universe for us to use starts with belief.* If you believe you can do something, then do it. If someone can talk you out of it, then you didn't believe. Don't allow the evil forces in life keep you where you don't want to be.

When David went against Goliath (1 Samuel 17), he believed that he could defeat this giant because David knew that he was tied into the power of God. David knew bringing down this giant who was the enemy would bring glory and honor to God. David even states:

"(45) Then David said to the Philistine, "You come to me with a sword, with a spear, and with a javelin. *But I come to you in the name of the Lord of hosts, the God of the armies of Israel, whom you have defied.* (46) This day the Lord will deliver you into my hand, and I will strike you and take your head from you. And this day I will give the carcasses of the camp of the Philistines to the birds of the air and the wild beasts of the earth, *that all the earth may know that there is a God* in Israel. (47) Then all this assembly shall know that the Lord does not save with sword and spear; for the battle is the Lord's, and He will give you into our hands."

We all have a Goliath in our life. Usually it is an addiction or a fear or a knuckling under to the life that we are living but really don't want to live. Right here, right now, I thank God for helping me slay my Goliaths. No matter how many times I try to take my Goliaths down by myself and fail, I realize some battles are not mine to fight. My journey is just as important as my accomplishing my goal and it is all good.

I have a Goliath in my life right now. I have been fighting this Goliath for nearly two years. I don't want the Goliath, and I wonder why I have not been relieved of this Goliath by my God? I have prayed about it, cursed my Goliath, I have done everything that I know to rid myself of my Goliath. My answer is in Romans chapter twelve verse nine. "My grace is sufficient for you." Leading up to this Scripture, we can read about the apostle Paul, who endured a Goliath of his own which was not removed from him. Paul reasoned that if his Goliath had been removed then he might possibly get a big head, and this was God's way of keeping him grounded. Most importantly, Paul did not allow his Goliath to cause him such anxiety that it would hinder him from continuing in his quest to further the gospel according to Jesus Christ. Therefore, he appreciated his Goliath because this Goliath could not stop him. The grace he received was enough to allow him to continue.

That is what we must do when we encounter our Goliaths: Continue on our journey of a positive existence, knowing that we too do not have to feel overwhelmed with anxiety and unworthiness. This is pretty powerful to not allow the negativity to hinder us from achieving our ultimate goal.

Chapter Ten

TOUGH LOVE

I feel like my brothers and sisters and I were raised in an atmosphere of tough love. When things were going well, it was the happiest time ever, but when we didn't agree with our parents, tough love was used. When I exhibit tough love with someone else, it is because I cannot be a part of enabling that person to continue down the road that they are traveling. That is the same thing my parents did to me. This type of reverse psychology or the *It's my way or the highway* didn't work on us. I cannot speak for my brothers and sisters, but if I was told that I was no good and I wouldn't amount to anything, I believed what I was told, and for many years I lived out the words that were spoken to me by my parents. I wish my parents knew the power that our words have and how they can affect people, especially your loved ones. These negative affirmations did not come often, and it wasn't beaten into my head, because I have very loving parents, but I believed those words were true.

Now, of course, I don't believe any negative sayings against me, and you can go use reverse psychology on someone else. Just be warned that if you tell your children that they are no good and they turn out no good, then you have yourself to thank for that. I know what you are thinking, *Oh, all my kids know that I love them. I do not have to tell them.* Yes, you do; it is your responsibility as a parent to raise your children in a loving environment, and regardless of what you believe they know, whether it's a child, brother, sister, spouse, mother, father, friend, uncle, aunt, grandmother, grandfather, … they all find it comforting and like to hear that they are loved.

I remember the talk I had with my parents as if it were yesterday, although it was many years ago. I'd finally had enough. Every idea I had wasn't good enough, and I was so sick and tired of hearing *You cannot do this or you cannot do that.* Finally, I told my parents, "What do you expect me to do, just lie down and die? If I can't accomplish anything in life, then what am I even living for? From now on, if you cannot add a positive remark, or if you tell me I will never amount to anything, then know that I am living out the words that you spoke over me."

After thinking for a moment, my father told me that I could do anything I set my mind to, and I have been going in a forward progressive motion ever since. It appears as though he did not want to be responsible for how my life ended up. A father's words to his children have the greatest impact on his children no matter how old they are. I have to admit even these trying talks that seemed so senseless to me happened for good. I got something out of it, and my parents got something out of it: We all learned the value of our words and their effect on people. That brings to mind the saying, *If you can't say something nice then don't say anything at all.*

I have come to find out that not all people know what tough love is or respond to tough love. As a matter of fact, tough love can have a reverse affect. Some people can believe that you are trying to be controlling, and they become very defensive. This just causes more division with the person you care about, and the end goal gets lost in the battle. It is very difficult to sit back and watch someone you care about make the same mistakes that you did and not be receptive to the knowledge that you have to offer. What do you do in a situation like this? First you remember that although most of us experience the same things in life, the journey we are all on is our own personal journey, and we all learn in our own way. The knowledge I have learned from the mistakes that I have made fit my life perfectly, and my journey has led me here. Your journey will lead you to the place that you need to be. So you can let go with the knowledge that the journey that you are on will bring you to the place that you need to be, that it will be beneficial to you because all things happen for good if we allow it. I will still offer some advice when I see you going in a questionable direction, but I will not get upset if you choose not to listen to what I am telling you.

When my parents did not agree with my decisions and knew I was making a mistake, they would talk to me. When I was not receptive to their advice, I was not bailed out of every bad decision that I made in life. When I chose to do things my way instead of how my parents suggested, they allowed me to go through what the outcome of my decisions were. It taught me accountability. I humbly say that I am grateful to my parents who did not save me from my incorrect decisions. Also I humbly say that when I made the right decisions, my parents were there with the positive accolades that I needed to continue to a life of success. All things did happen for good.

If you really want to know what tough love is all about, look at God and his love for us. With all the terrible things going on in the world today, it is amazing that the entire human race has not been wiped off the face of the earth. I do believe that God has found a way to love each and every one of us on a personal level despite our actions, and believe me, that is what tough love is all about. There still is a lot of good people in the world and each of us has goodness inside of us. I believe it is because of the good people who have the faith and belief in God that we are still here. It is our job to bring glory and honor to God by our actions and by our words. Each and every person has a purpose in life to show that the world is good and can get better by believing in this higher power who would like for us to excel in abundance.

It is totally amazing to me how many different realities there are in life. A whole crowd of people can witness a situation and come up with different views of what went on. I think that this is awesome; someone who has an opinion of what happened might be different than my opinion. Hearing their opinion gives me a different perspective on what is happening. I can agree with them or I can disagree with them. The choice is mine to make; I must admit, though, many times my opinion has changed when I got another person's perspective. Seeing things from someone else's perspective is life changing. It brings you experience and expands your mental capacity above seeing life with our own set of personal blinders on. One thing is for sure: I am not going to get upset or defensive when someone chooses not to see things my way. They have the right to see things their own way.

I have come to find out that there is a tremendous amount of people that believe life is a series of negative events that we must live through and then you die. They live their life with this tough love philosophy, and they teach their children this tough love philosophy. Some parents believe that it is a cruel world out there and they have to toughen their child up to be prepared for what is coming. There is some truth to this tough love philosophy. There will be good times, and there will be bad times. We will love life and we will hate life – or even worse, we will get stuck living in a dark hole called mental illness such as depression or an eating disorder. Now even tough love will not work. People talk with other people like them who experience the same symptoms, and they are validated in their belief that this is just the way life is. *No one who doesn't have this same mental illness can understand; they just don't know what it is like to be me living with this disease.* You are right, and good luck with that. Go and live your life the way you feel most comfortable and let me know how that works out for you.

If by chance you would like to talk about it, then I am going to tell you because of the studies that I did I have found out that we are creators of our own life. We can choose to live a life of happiness with good and positive things that happen to us all the time, no matter what disease we are living with. The depression, anxiety, eating disorder and every other mental illness can be gone or in remission with the power that is free for us to use. It is the belief and the faith that holds the cure. I am not suggesting that people stop taking their medication for what ails them, but I am suggesting that you can be cured with faith and belief that the love of God wants you to be cured because that would be a testament to His power, which in turn would bring God the glory and honor he deserves.

Oh sure, there will be bad things that happen to us – of course it will be more advantageous if we allow this thought to come into our minds. Maybe some good will come out of this bad thing, is that even possible? I mean, going through this bad thing with these bad feelings is rough. I cannot even pretend to like what is going on. I agree with you, I hate going through bad things more than anybody. My God, I lived in misery my whole life and you know what? I am done with misery. Say that out loud. "I am done with living a miserable life. I choose to live a positive, faith-filled life. I am grateful to God for bringing me through this terrible experience, and I know all things happen for good, even the bad things in life, to those who love God and are called according to his purpose." You don't even have to believe those words, but I know for a fact that you will get past the bad experience quicker, and you don't have to be a victim of life. Also as a bonus if you say those words out loud enough times you will come to believe that you too are called according to God's purpose and it is all good.

    I know how difficult it is to go through bad times. I have been through enough of them. I also see myself exhibiting this tough love philosophy toward the people that I love and care for dearly. It is almost a battle of wills in some cases, and a division or a wall has gotten built between us. Well, I don't want the wall there, and I won't enable you, or bail you out of any trouble that you get yourself into, especially since I am so wrong and you are so right and I will pray and believe that God can take your negative situation and turn it around for good. I trust that you will figure it out, hopefully sooner rather than later.

    Sometimes I think that the only one who knows what real tough love is about is God. The number of times have I personally done a wrong to God and only God has to be in the millions. I do not know the correct number, but I am sure it is astronomical. Yet every day *I know that God still loves me*. If someone did me wrong that many times, I admit it would be hard for me to love that someone. So it would seem to me that in order for God to love me, it must be tough. In reality, though, it is not tough for God to love me because God is Love. It is a character trait of God; it is what God does. This is not a permission slip to say that you can do whatever you want and God will still love you because it says in the Bible that you should not tempt the Lord your God. In other words, God has no problem taking you down a peg or two to make you realize that He will not be taken for granted.

When you do a wrong to God or to anybody, the first thing in our nature to do is to try to get away from God or that someone. We sort of give up. *Well, I did wrong to God again. I fell into that same addiction I have been trying to get away from, and I am ashamed. I know this time God will not answer my prayer. God probably hates me by now.* We convince ourselves that we are not lovable or deserving of forgiveness. We decide that God will not love us or that God will not answer our prayers. In all actuality, we should be running to God. We should get it out in the open. *Okay, God, I humbly come to You. We both know I did You wrong again. I am sorry, and whatever punishment You have for me is understandable just as long as I can get back in Your good graces. By the way, I don't seem to be able to stop this addiction, anger issue, drinking etc… but I believe in my heart that You can free me, and when the time is right I will no longer have this issue that apparently I cannot get away from on my own. Please send help.* From this point on your prayer is answered in God's timing. Believe it!

Chapter Eleven

GRATITUDE

I wake up in the morning thanking God. It has become a natural reflex. I yawn, stretch, and say, *Thank you God for all the blessings that you will give me today.* God has proven to me by His actions that He is the most loving, forgiving, merciful, kindest, powerful and giving. The most important of my daily rituals is to thank God and believe you me, if I am with you I am quick to point out if a blessing happens. I want God to see that I am paying attention to Him. I mean, after all, I couldn't accomplish all that I have accomplished without the supernatural nudge in the right direction, the meeting of the right person, the lining up of everything in the universe. I am calling in the blessings and using the free power of God that is here for everybody. I really don't believe in coincidences at all. When you think about the vastness of the universe and how there is something going on at every second of the day, how can there be coincidences? A coincidence to me is you are at the same store at the same time as one of your friends, but on a personal level meeting the exact person that you needed to meet for something important is more than a coincidence: It is a blessing.

    I know what you are thinking: *Well, that really hasn't been my experience. I haven't got the breaks that you have gotten, and I think God may be taking care of someone else or I am not worthy to get that nudge in the right direction. I went to Walmart and had to park way down there at the end of the parking lot and walk forever because I never can find that perfect parking spot, my kids don't like me, my dog bit me three times last week, my boss hates me, and my wife burns all the TV dinners. I won't even mention that I got three bald tires on my rusted-out pickup truck, my grass won't grow, mostly the bills get paid, some a little late, and I'm losing my hair and getting fat. If God is as great as you say, why is my life so bad?*

Well, I could give you some tough love truth there, but you wouldn't like me afterwards or I could tell you that you are very blessed. You see, God is a purposeful God. All the bad things in your life may be a wakeup call from God for you to straighten out your life. God uses the underprivileged people of the world. If you go back and read the Old Testament, you will find case after case of what I am talking about. Just to name a few: Moses was a murderer and a fugitive for forty years, and he led the Hebrews out of Egypt; David was a shepherd boy, and he became king; Rahab was a prostitute who hid a couple spies and lied to the King of Jericho about it, and Rahab ended up in the family line of Jesus. In the New Testament, some of the apostles were blue collar workers (fishermen) who cussed, were prone to fighting and drank, but Peter became the cornerstone of the church. James and John were known as "the brothers thunder," and they went on to a write some of the books of the Bible. My point is that like you, these people did not have perfect lives. Every one did things wrong – not only that, I am sure they went through some difficulties. Only a few people remember God during the good times. We think we only need God when things are going bad, otherwise we got it from here. There are some verses in the Bible that were written by King David where he is giving us insight as to why his life is so successful, and he wants to share his knowledge and experience. The verses that I speak of go like this: "Oh, give thanks to the Lord! [King David is just saying to give credit where credit is due.] Call upon His name [Rely on God]; Make known His deeds among the peoples! [Let others know how your prayers were answered] 9 Sing to Him, sing psalms to Him; Talk of all His wondrous works! [In this we remember God's helpfulness and if we are recalling all the good God has done for us, our mind is positive.] 10 Glory in His holy name; Let the hearts of those rejoice who seek the Lord! [Because we found the secret to happiness] 11 Seek the Lord and His strength; Seek His face evermore! [This keeps negativity out of our lives.] 12 Remember His marvelous works which He has done, His wonders, and the judgments of His mouth." God keeps his promises, but how many people keep a record of all the good things God has done for them and visit that record often?

Essentially, King David is saying if you follow this advice you will have a blessed and happy life just like him. I am not the type of person who goes around and forces my religious beliefs on people. I have realized that we are living in a world where it can have a reverse effect on people if you try to convince them of your beliefs verbally. This is where the way you live your life is a greater testament than anything you can say verbally. I could not understand why certain priests and ministers were so happy, and I was so miserable. What did they have that I didn't have? They had it all: happiness, the right breaks, they were financially secure, these people wanted to help people, and they were filled with such gratitude. It was unbelievable, so naturally I wanted that.

I remember a time when I was working at a thrift store and the place was gloomy. Nobody talked to each other, or the conversation was minimal. And it was just a somber place to work. I never preached about the power that was available to them to live a happy blessed life. I just went about my business. I helped out and went the extra mile, and before long the place was more cheerful, and people would be more apt to help one another. My actions were contagious. I would give rides home to some of my co-workers in the wintertime, and during one of these times my co-worker confided in me that he hated me for the first month that I worked there.

"Why is that?" I inquired.

"Because you are always so happy, and you are not like everyone else I know."

Well, I stated that I choose to be happy, and the look I got from him was pure astonishment. He did not understand that happiness is a choice. I got the impression from him that in order to be happy everything in life would have to go your way. Let's face it, life doesn't work that way, but you can still choose to be happy amid all the chaos. I am sure he is still thinking about that statement.

If you are waiting for everything to go your way in order to be happy, then get used to your life now because what you have done is placed the power of your choice in a world full of dissention. It is not always easy to be happy, but I hope like me you will choose to be happy no matter what is going on. You are not in charge of anybody's happiness, and nobody is in charge of your happiness. Make the choice to be happy. When bad times come, allow yourself to feel your emotions, don't deny them, but then put down those emotions. Thank God for the experience knowing all things happen for good because that is what you choose to believe, then choose and pick up where you left off on your mission to be full of gratitude, happiness, and all things positive. You are in control, and you are the creator of your life.

"Be anxious for nothing, but in everything by prayer and supplication, with thanksgiving, let your requests be made known to God; 7 and the peace of God, which surpasses all understanding, will guard your hearts and minds through Christ Jesus." (Philippians 4:6,7) Here we are taught to have thanksgiving as we pray – why? Why is it so important to have thanksgiving? With thanksgiving comes a positive connotation that you believe that God has your best interest at heart. It keeps your mind off the negative that can grow out of control very quickly.

I know what you are thinking: *I am sorry, I just can't be thankful for some of the things that are going on in my life.* I do understand; we are but human beings, and we are on a path to a destination. We must allow ourselves to feel the emotions that we are feeling, but if you continue to feel un-thankfulness, there is a chance the list of things not to believe God can turn around for good can grow to many things, and that means that you have already made up your mind and choose not to believe that all things happen for good to those who love God and are called according to His purpose.

I feel like I was closer to my mother than I was with my dad. In my mother's last years, she developed lung cancer, and I was devastated. I couldn't see how anything good can come out of lung cancer, and to be honest I was not done with my mom in this life yet. I needed her for the moral support that only a mother can give her son, and to be honest I believed that she needed me just as she needed all her grown-up kids. My mother's unconditional love was outstanding. I mean, she knew how to give it even when she did not agree with the choices that her children made, and she let you know it, too.

My mother went through chemo and radiation treatments, and I believe they got the lung cancer under control. Unfortunately, the treatments stopped her from being able to swallow food and keep that food down, so she just got weaker and weaker, and the pain she was in was unbearable to her, not to mention all of her kids who watched her die. We are talking some serious pain here for all of us, especially my mom, who was loved dearly. Finally one day I couldn't take seeing my mother like this and I started crying like a three-year-old. I heard my mother say, "Hey don't worry I can live for another ten years."

Through my tears I told her that I didn't want her to. I wanted her to go be with my dad and move on and that it was just too rough to see her in so much pain. I told her that she was a great mother and we would be okay. I told my mother it was okay for her to move on; she'd fulfilled her purpose in life by raising her kids right.

You see, I believe my mother was hanging on for me. She was dead set on fulfilling her purpose of being the mother that I needed her to be no matter how much pain and agony she was in. She wouldn't let go until her last bit of strength was gone. I was very selfish up until that point when the tears came. I suppose in my subconscious I knew we had to let my mother move on. She died later that night, and I have no regrets about what I said to her. She was free to go, and she believed me.

I was sure that I was going to be a complete mess after my mother's passing, but I was not a mess. I believe that her strength lives on in me, and I am strong and determined. There is no better compliment that I could give to her than to live my life in the way that I am living. I am sure my mother and father are looking down and saying, *I sure am proud of that kid. He is a doer, and he loves God just like we wanted.* I don't believe in the statement that when someone dies that they are no longer with us. Oh sure, I will have to go to them eventually, but my loved ones are with me all the time.

Plenty of good came out of a very sad situation where I believed no good could. I do miss giving my mom and dad physical hugs, but the good outweighs the bad. Because of my beliefs, I really didn't have to search too hard for the good. My mother is no longer in pain, and she made me promise that the road I am traveling down I will keep going with full steam ahead. We, her children, get along a little better now – at least we try a little more. My mother is not forgotten; she shows up just at the right times in our minds with the atta boy. The peace of God which surpasses all understanding did and still does guard my heart and mind just like God promised.

Chapter Twelve

DEDICATION

How dedicated are you to your own life? Do you love yourself? When you describe yourself, are you selling yourself short or making fun of yourself? Do you consider yourself worthy to have a good life? What do you believe about you? Are you grateful? Do you see the blessings that come to you every day?

My answers are that I am very dedicated to my life. I love myself tremendously, I am a God fearing, morally upstanding, ethically solid, loyal beyond belief, empathetic, good-looking man who is probably the most grateful person you will ever meet. I am self-aware, non-judgmental, humble, and always willing to learn to become a better person. I am a good listener and I always go in a forward progressive motion. When my heart calls for it, I am always willing to help others, and I am full of unconditional love and giving. Considering my life and where I came from I am totally worthy to have a good life, and I will not accept anything less. I believe I am going forward, and that there is no one who can stop me (except for myself) and I am very grateful for the blessings that I receive from God each and every day. I rely on God's blessings and I am dependent on His free power to get me to where I need to go. I also know that I am not perfect. I make mistakes, and there is room for improvement. I am grateful for my shortcomings because they make me who I am. I also know if I was perfect then I would no longer have a reason to go forward.

I know what you are thinking: *Wow, this guy is really full of himself*, but in reality, I am full of appreciation to God for who He made me to be. Some people can just whip through life and succeed at everything that they touch. I am not one of those people. Yet I am smart enough to know that there is power in the universe that I can tap into to help me achieve my goals. I know that there is power in me, in what I say to myself and to others that will help me live the life that I want to live and create the life that I want to create. I also know that it starts and ends with believing the impossible is no longer impossible. Years ago it was impossible to fly to the moon, yet that became a reality. It was impossible to overcome the many plagues that existed until someone set out to achieve the impossible and created vaccines to keep people alive. It was impossible to be cured from many illnesses until someone believed and was dedicated enough to do the research to become a doctor and heal. The world is so full of impossibilities that I am not shocked when another achievement is accomplished.

To many people I know and to many people I see in the world, it is an impossibility to get passed their past and move on. They don't believe that they can, and they accept that this is who they are and how things will always be. I believe that they can do it. I've heard it said that God is everywhere – well, if that is the case then so is the power of God that can bring healing and change to everyone who is dedicated enough get a handle on their negative emotions and thoughts and to always go in a forward progressive motion. Also just like the woman who believed that if she touched Jesus then she would be healed, you too can tap into this power from God that is free for the taking. Remember it was her faith that made her well, not the actual touching which represented her faith. I guarantee if you live your life in a positive fashion you too will want to go in a forward progressive motion for the rest of your life.

When I look around this world and see the hatred, the greed, the immorality, the unforgiveness, and the unwillingness to change, I can't help but think to fix this is an impossibility. But I quickly suppress those negative thoughts because I believe in the power of God to fix what is wrong. I wonder how we got here. How did we lose our belief in this country? Well, we changed. We created the life that we now live, and there are many great and positive things going on this world, but there are many things that are not so great. My question is why can't we change again?

The change of the world starts on a personal level. The world will go in the direction of the people who inhabit it. If you raise your children in a positive environment, they will grow up to be positive. If you raise your children to be believers then they will be believers. If you raise your children to be responsible they will be responsible.

It was said in the Old Testament and repeated in the New Testament by the Apostle Peter in his first epistle chapter three, "He who would love life And see good days, Let him refrain his tongue from evil, And his lips from speaking deceit." Are you dedicated enough to your own life to refrain your tongue from evil, to stop complaining about how your life is and how other people are? Are you dedicated enough to your own life to concentrate on creating the life that you would like for yourself? I hear people complain all the time about their co-workers and how they are lazy and irresponsible and how they would not act like that. I have a question: Would you like everybody in the world to be like you? Exactly the same, no variety, no free will. I am not condoning laziness – I believe everyone should pitch in and help get the job done – but what is most important is when you lay your head down at night do you feel like you did the best that you could have regardless of who you work with? "And let us not grow weary while doing good, for in due season we shall reap if we do not lose heart." (Galatians 6:9) This verse is telling us specifically not to give up when something does not happen when you want it to happen. You will be rewarded for doing the right thing.

Dedication to oneself is not a one-day adventure. We will always experience trouble and downfalls. Trouble and downfalls should be looked at as our growing season; it allows us to see how far we have come on our journey. Dedication is not sweating the small stuff; dedication is when a negative thought comes to mind, we don't concentrate on the negative thought, we don't speak the negative thought, we don't worry about the negative thought, and we certainly don't act on the negative thought. We take that negative thought and we tell ourselves, *That is enough of that. I will not allow this negative though to control me any longer. I am blessed, I am happy, and I am grateful for all the good in my life, and I choose to continue down the path that I am meant to go down. I was born to be filled with love, and I will live abundantly."*

I cannot tell you the amount of times someone has paid me a compliment, and my response was a negative. For example, someone would say, "Wow, Jim, you are a very handsome man." My response would be, "No" – as if I did not believe them – "I have gained a few too many pounds and I could look better." Or someone would tell me, "You are awesome," and I would say, "No, I'm just me. I am nobody special." Now my response is, "Thank you for noticing." I humbly say, "I thank God for making me this way." God did such a great job that other people are noticing. When I pay you a compliment, please realize that God put it in me to see this great attribute in you. Also who am I to get in the way of what someone else thinks of me? On the other hand, if you think bad thoughts of me, please keep them to yourself. I don't need your negative comments, and I believe if you are thinking about what a bad person I am, it must be you are ashamed of yourself and you don't want anybody analyzing you.

We all have the same destination in life. How we get to that destination is how we choose to live. I am dedicated enough to my life to go through hardships and feel the emotions that come with that hardship until I recognize that these emotions are hindering me from progressing. I truly believe that hardships are a blessing now, and I thank God for the hardship because I know something good will come out of it. You too can choose to believe all things happen for good, and I hope you do. That does not mean that you will never feel the pain of hurt, but that there is a light at the end of the tunnel, and you will come out better than when you went in.

I know what you are thinking: *Well, I prayed and prayed, and none of my prayers were ever answered. I guess God must be busy with something else, and I just do not matter. So why should I be as dedicated as you say? Why should I waste all my time with all this positive stuff that you are talking about when bad things are just always going to happen? Besides, you don't know what you are talking about. Look at the world there is so much turmoil and hatred that is in it. I don't know anybody that has a life that it easy.*

I know what you are talking about. I was the same as you in my thinking, and actually I was probably worse. It took me years to get past my past, but that is exactly what the past is – it is past; it is over. I found that as long as I kept looking back at what I did and what prayers went unanswered, I could not see where I was going. I also found that *I was the reason* why I was not receiving the blessings or the good breaks that I figured that I should get. One thing that you can count on is that you will never live a blessed life with a negative attitude. You will not receive the positive when you live in the negative.

Chapter Thirteen

CONCLUSION

How would you feel if you knew that one of your close and trusted friends who has been with you for years is going to do you wrong, not once or twice but three times or more? I know what you are thinking: *Well, that wouldn't be my friend for very long!* Friends don't do friends wrong. I think back to my mother. If you did her wrong one time that's it buddy, you were done. "I don't need people who do me wrong in my life," she would say. She would grace her children with a couple more chances, but the threat was always looming there like a buzzard waiting for their prey to die. I am sure my mom gave everybody multiple chances – after all, she was a very loving woman, but it was very disconcerting to know that at any moment if you unintentionally did something wrong you were done.

The Apostle Peter did Jesus wrong, and Christ even told him that he would. It is a funny thing being human; we know ourselves pretty well and what we will do in any given situation, but for some reason the way we should act is not how we actually do act. In the book of Matthew, Christ explained to his disciples that all of them would be made to stumble. Peter in his ultimate wisdom specifically states, "Even if all are made to stumble because of you, I will never be made to stumble." (Matthew 26:33) Peter went on to say that he would die before he denied Christ, and all the disciples reaffirmed what Peter said. I have seen this many times in my life when friends promised to stick by each other till death, but it did not work out that way. The big difference was that Jesus knew that Peter was human, and humans make mistakes. Jesus also knew that Peter had a pure heart, and Jesus looks at our hearts even when we make mistakes.

The story goes on that when Jesus was betrayed by Judas and was taken away, Peter followed along and was warming himself by the fire when he was recognized. Naturally, Peter denied knowing Jesus and left. That sounds pretty human; when you are accused of something, you deny it and leave. Well, it happened again Peter was recognized, and of course Peter denied it. He saw what was going on with Jesus and the crowd was in an agitated state. Peter had to deny it or else he could have suffered the same fate as Jesus. Peter, along with the other apostles, had just spent three years with Jesus, witnessing miracle after miracle, being taught and mentored by Jesus himself. Peter was supposed to be the stone on which the church was built, the leader of the apostles, one of the inner circle of Jesus' friends (along with James and John). Everyone knows about Saint Peter at the gates of heaven. This guy Peter had one honor after another; after all, he was handpicked by Jesus to be an apostle. Yet that third time he was recognized, this man of honor, this stone, this protector, this leader, this committed to Christ until death man reverted right back to his fisherman days. He swore and cussed out the people who said that he was one of Jesus' disciples.

Yes, Peter and the other disciples did Jesus terrible wrong. That is not the worst part of the story. The worst part is that Jesus went on to be crucified, and Peter, along with the others, did not have a chance to apologize for their betrayal. I am sure that was one big regret that they were feeling. Would you like to do someone wrong and not have a chance to apologize? Not only that; they probably wondered if Jesus was the Christ. After all, Jesus said that he would never leave them. There had to be some doubt and what should they do now? Waiting to see what would happen next was driving them crazy, so Peter said he was going back to fishing. He was a fisherman, and he would go back to what he knew. His partners came with them, and they fished all night with no luck.

When morning came, Jesus yelled to them, "Children, have you any food?" (John 21:5) "No," they replied, and he said, "Cast your net on the right side of the boat." (John 21:6)

When they did, they caught one hundred and fifty-three fish. This was actually more than their nets could handle, yet the nets did not break. When you think about it that is pretty funny. Here they'd fished all night without a catch all because the fish were on the other side of the boat. Their abundance was right there – not down in another lake or the other side of the street, but with them the whole time.

The disciples knew that Jesus was on the shore, and Peter jumped out of the boat in his exuberance to get back to Christ. This might be his only chance to apologize for his betrayal. The thing that matters is that he ran to Christ, not away from Christ like when we do something wrong and we feel like we will have to live with this guilt forever. We can be restored just as Peter was restored. This story is so important to us because it teaches us that when we have guilt we need to clear the air instead of living with this negative emotion. You cannot move forward in a negative state, and with time you can be restored. If you are dealing with a personal friend or relative who rejects your apology, then at least you know that you did what you could to make amends. You are not in control of anybody else's feelings, and you cannot make someone accept your apology, but you can move forward. Hopefully time will heal any wounds, and all will be okay. One thing is for sure: All things happen for good if you want them to. Another important part of this story is that Christ is right there to help you clear the air. You don't have to go looking for him, and he is a prayer away no matter where you are.

The author

James Kubik came from a troubled past. Through his desire to overcome negativity and find happiness, he began an in-depth study of the Bible and discovered the keys to happiness through the power that God has put in place to assist us.

You are welcome to contact the author at jbuk153@gmail.com.

novum PUBLISHER FOR NEW AUTHORS

The publisher

*He who stops
getting better
stops being good.*

This is the motto of novum publishing, and our focus is on finding new manuscripts, publishing them and offering long-term support to the authors.
Our publishing house was founded in 1997, and since then it has become THE expert for new authors and has won numerous awards.

Our editorial team will peruse each manuscript within a few weeks free of charge and without obligation.

You will find more information about
novum publishing and our books on the internet:

www.novumpublishing.com

novum 🔔 PUBLISHER FOR NEW AUTHORS

Rate this book on our website!

www.novumpublishing.com

www.ingramcontent.com/pod-product-compliance
Lightning Source LLC
Chambersburg PA
CBHW022109160426
43198CB00008B/403